REVELATION

ISBN 979-8-89383-532-8

REVELATION

WHERE WE ARE AT IN BIBLE PROPHECY

MINISTER DERRICK LACY

CONTENTS

Introduction   vii

PART ONE

1. Signs and Symbols   3
2. The Truth   9
3. Head of Gold   18
4. The Great Controversy (Satan Vs Christ)   22
5. How Satan Joined The Church   34
6. The Roead That Leads To Heaven   36
7. Angel-Messenger   59
8. Church of Ephesus (Rev.2:1)   64

PART TWO

9. A Whole New World   101
10. Today's Reading   105

INTRODUCTION

"Revelation" in Greek or Hebrew means "That which is revealed". It's our "End Time Message" given to us by Jesus, which the angel shared with Saint John, who did what the Spirit told him by giving it to the Body of Christ. It's a forecast which depicts the events leading up to Jesus' Second Coming. Giving us exact footage of the conduct of the good and bad. Sad to say, But many pastors, preachers, and teachers will try and tell the church with its body of believers that it's a closed book based on scriptures taken out of context (Dan. 12:4). But, If we were to read this scripture in its entirety it would reveal that the prophecy would be open to us when the end time is near or here. Some pastors convey that it's a book of mysteries not to be understood at all. In comparison, we'll see that Daniel and Revelation go hand in hand, and they're both simple to understand in revealing where we are in bible prophecy through understanding the scriptures. Jesus would want us to have the breast of the facts about what manner the chips are to lay or fall, so to speak. Mathew 24 gives us a good description of the voice of Jesus that reaches our current generation of events. It's not hidden to those of us who are striving for the knowledge of the whole truth, which is vital to keep us from losing our crown (2 Corinth. 4:4, 1 Corinth. 2:9, 10). It's raining! Raining all over the world, and many of us are caught in it without our umbrellas! The Bible says too much; who is given much is required! So, let this be an introduction of me beginning to teach us "End Time Prophecy Through The Scriptures."

The Apostle John, who was one of the twelve who walked and talked with Jesus during His term on earth, was given a "Prophetic Word" from God, signified by the angel of the Lord. John was considered the one that Jesus loved the most. John was one of The Sons of Zebedee, along with his brother James. The Zebedees were well off and shared in their family business with their dad as fishermen. They followed the calling of Jesus and excused themselves from working with their father to pursue a higher calling with hands-on experience. We can recall that Brother John was there for just about every major event or supernatural scene, along with Peter and James. John was the one leaning on Jesus or in His bosom around the fire. John was the one Jesus trusted to take care of His mother, Mary, as He instructed before He gave up the ghost. All the other disciples became martyrs, but John's fate was decided by sending him to a deserted island to silence his testimony after the death of Mary. Those who opposed the gospel silenced the disciples by killing them. For some reason, they chose to exile Saint John to an island called Patmos. John stayed tuned to The Spirit and caught God's Message on one Sabbath Day (Rev.1:10). The angel told him three important things that should begin a ray of confidence about one looking into this book of prophecy (Rev.1:3). Tell us that we will be blessed to hear, read (Meaning with understanding) and keep this prophecy. So, We see here that knowing is half the battle, and we are to act according to what we know to be effective in keeping ourselves out of harm's way. Jesus makes it known by what manner His Second Coming is and the conditions that surround it. Let Us be prepared because the time is near.Rev.1:3...for the time is near (K.J.V), (Daniel 2:21, 22).

PART ONE

CHAPTER 1
SIGNS AND SYMBOLS

Signs and symbols are used as visual aids to give us a mental picture of what it's describing. So, this appeals to what one puts in or on one's mind.

Note: The mind (brain) is the eye-gate to our soul, and it can and will determine where our soul will spend eternity.

With this being said, we must watch what we allow ourselves to be entertained with.

Garbage in/Garbage out. Our brain, through what the eyes see, is recorded instantly, whether we are aware of it or not. We call it "Subliminal Messages". The sub-conscience level (what we are unlikely to be aware of) is the most powerful level of our mind. This means that we're more prone to act out on the things that our mind takes unawares. And through the process level," Mind/Heart," a thing or action can be born. Example: Evil thoughts as a thought pattern exercised will become matters of the heart, leading to hard habits to break! That's why, to have victory in this area, we need to be on guard! (Prov. 4:23).

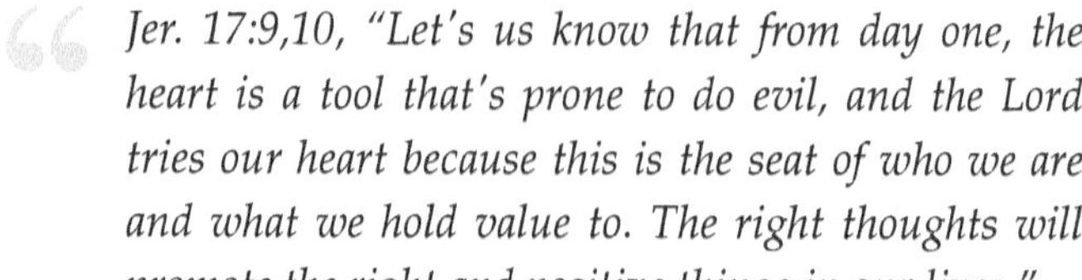

> *Jer. 17:9,10, "Let's us know that from day one, the heart is a tool that's prone to do evil, and the Lord tries our heart because this is the seat of who we are and what we hold value to. The right thoughts will promote the right and positive things in our lives."*

Phil. 4:7, 8 gives us an edge on a successful thought life when we apply this. Please read it before going further. Revelation is a book that holds many signs and symbols to help us get the message at hand, with us taking time out to piece together things like a puzzle. Our attention span must be intact in order to detect the message like a puzzle. It's required of one to take time out with patience. And like many whose attention span is short, they don't pursue puzzles or reading books. In short, one has to be willing to go further than just on the surface level for this kind of message. It requires one to dig deeper. God was careful to protect this "Prophetic Message" with signs and symbols. Through a deeper and sincere relationship, He's made it known to those who will pass it on.

As we continue to proceed to discover where we are at in bible prophecy, I would like to impose a thought to consider all through this lesson study. Let us unlearn so that we can learn. This means everything that is taught in the scriptures that we just took for granted and that was passed down in certain denominations. Let it fly or be investigated in light of the scriptures not being taken out of context.

For example: Once Saved / Always Saved. Matt 7:15-23, Rev. 2:5, 22:19. These verses leave no room for compromise. Let's put what we've been taught (not to say that it was false) on the back burner as we study. We must unlearn in most cases so we can learn. We see here in *Revelations* that there are seven churches that make up the Asia Minor that actually existed. But let's use our spiritual scope as if the Holy Spirit had it. The Spirit of The Lord would acknowledge their good works (The Churches) and their shortcomings as well. And just like any born-again spirit-filled church or body of believers, there's going to be room for improvement in looking through the Eyes of The Lord! And we know that the Eyes of the Lord or upon the righteous (1 Peter 3:12, 2 Chron. 16:9). We know that The Lord does things decently and in order (1Corinth. 14:40). Also, Our Heavenly Father gives us space to repent as spoken in Rev. 2:5 and He always sends warnings before judgment. This is the very nature of God, who wishes none of us to perish with the goat. Hell, it will be full of people with good intentions! Those who were sincere but sincerely wrong! So, let's start taking steps to secure our soul's salvation by paying close attention to the warning signs! The churches stem from 1 to 7. Prophetically, Church number seven represents the church in its fullness of time. God's "Last Day" Church or the church that appears at the end of time, which is us. We are in the last of the last days in which we all can agree, right? All messages apply to us as God's Church among the seven, but The Church of Laodiceans is The Body of Christ in these last days. This is a specific message to us as the church, and it definitely depicts our character. I would like to pause for now to let this marinate, and we will get to the meat and potatoes in the next episode.

The Church is a body of believers who have accepted The Death, Burial, and Resurrection of Jesus Christ. We are to exercise the life of Christ through our resurrected life. The world of lost souls is to view us as someone they can get an image of Christ-likeness. We, as the church, are to set the world on fire with the message of salvation and get to a place where we can teach along spiritual guidelines. But there is a thing I've seen in the church, and that is that many pastors are stuck on preaching! Preaching is designed to lead the sinner to Christ to a born-again experience and the saint to repentance from living corrupt. Then, once they're in the church, teach them The Word and how to live a victorious life here on earth. Then, if we've been taught through experience, we can share our knowledge. May we share what we've learned if it is well with our souls. We can learn from the examples of the seven churches mentioned here in *Revelations*, which was a body of believers in the past. The Word compels us to take into consideration those things done by our forefathers in the bible as a warning (1 Corth. 10:6,11). We are going to take note of the things these seven churches were doing to make history, their good and bad or falling short.

R *evelations* is our end-time message forecasting what is and what is to be in this era we live in now. This prophecy at a percentage is about 80% fulfilled, as we will see. Matthew 24th Chp. Gives us an account from the very lips of Jesus, a forecast of earthquakes in various places. And we can testify to this, seeing that we've been experiencing this even in our own backyards for those of us who are in TX. This is to name just one state, but we can give an account of this happening in other states where history has it happening. Major catastrophes, such as mudslides, avalanches, forest fires, etc., have made their way into our headlines, just to name a few. And who can forget about the many floods that have wiped out many homes along with people and their pets? It also states (Jesus speaking) that the condition of wars would be rumors. It is just rumors because we can't put much emphasis on what the media is bringing to us. I say this because we know or ought to know that the media wants to control our thinking to allow us to be dictated to. This is to control and manipulate our decision-making. In short, We can't or shouldn't take to heart everything the news brings to our attention. With God, through the person of Jesus, regulating our minds and being on the throne of our hearts, we can govern ourselves accordingly. Jesus also lets us know the condition of the church by saying the hearts of many will wax cold. This is directly to those of us who were once on fire for the Lord. For one's heart to get too cold below freezing (wax), it shows that its first state was hot. And this is what Jesus says would be at this hour. He says that when we see things taking place, we should not be alarmed because the end is not yet here. This gives us a probation period or grace period to line up to meet the master. This is a time to take advantage of the space to repent. Let's get our house in order so that we can be presented without a spot or flaw!

***

What will one do in exchange for the truth? Or are there people who are motivated by the truth on a small or larger scale? There are many definitions or meanings for every word that is formed or in the Webster's dictionary. These many words can reflect a poor meaning or lesser meaning in the Light of God's Word, The Bible. Outside of God's Word and Webster's dictionary, one can form or draw their own opinion.

Example: Love? In the light of the scriptures, it means an unconditional love that shows action without a hidden agenda or strings attached. A love that comes from God with one acting out the born-again experience, which is not selfish. In the words of the woman who had a son who died as she addressed the prophet Elijah: "Now, by this, I know that you are a man of God and that the word of the Lord in your mouth is the truth." 1 Kings 17:24.

The Truth being spoken by a person of God (Christians) is a sure way to identify one as a Child of God. The truth is handled poorly in the courtrooms when one is asked to raise one's right hand with these words. Do you promise to tell the whole truth and nothing but the truth, so help you, God?

CHAPTER 2
THE TRUTH

The Truth is what is under attack in our quest for freedom. This is what everything that God stands for rests upon. Many will conceal The Truth to embrace a Lie. This has come naturally since The Fall of Man. A Lie is what 1/3 of the angels believed that got them hurled out of Heaven. And since then, Satan has told a lie to maintain control over the lives of us as humans. It's more popular to lie in today's society; that gives it strength because many have a secret identity that they don't won't expose. Please believe that one white lie, as it is called, can bust hell wide open in the lives of those who exercise their right to do so, which has deceived many as well as themselves. No one living a lie likes to be exposed or put out in the open because of shame.

So, let us embrace the truth the first time and make it a diet of things in our lives so we can feel good about ourselves all the time. Many self-righteous organizations have built their foundation on lies masquerading as the truth that will only be revealed on Judgment Day unless we, as The Body of Christ, do our part to save them from The Wrath of God.

Matthew 5:6, We are called Blessed of the Lord when we go whole-heartily after the truth. And our reward is being filled with the truth and what it has to offer. Verse 14 Lets us know that we are The Light of the World, which means The truth because Truth exposes darkness or that which is hidden because of darkness. We are Light bearers or vessels that can channel The Word of God. Light helps us to see by exposing a Lie. To know the truth about something is to be enlightened. So, Light and Truth are for the same purpose. Darkness blinds, Falsehood and Lies blind; Keep covered. Verse 15 Can read like this:

> *No one lights a lamp and then puts it under a covering that can keep it from shining or bringing light to things on the surface. So, those who know the truth about things but, for whatever reason, keep it covered or to themselves (not sharing), when sharing, can get us out of darkness so we can see. By seeing this, we can make better decisions because we can see the pitfalls.*

Romans 1:8 says that God's Anger is made known to us from above against all things contrary to His True Identity, which is being of truth. This is, in my own words, made to describe what this verse is saying. Verse 18, revealed from heaven, means it has reached heaven and got God's attention. Which, in other words, means God has to do something about it. The unrighteousness of men who suppress (Twist or Add to; Hide or Keep Covered) The Truth for selfish motives. Verse 19 says: At one time, they were positioned to know and receive God's Truth that He gave to them as a witness.

As we reflect on the condition of the 1st. The Church mentioned (Church of Ephesus) in *Revelation* we, as the Church of Christ, can identify with being in a backsliding condition. However it came to be, it's a feeling of being totally lost and eaten up with guilt! But let us be reminded that God is married to the backsliders who were us at one time in the past. (Jeremiah 3:14)

Consequences: Rev. 2:5- I will come quickly and remove your lampstand from its place. There's nothing more horrifying than being in a backsliding condition where the anointing has left one! Immediately, our minds are so under attack that we are quick to believe a lie that we're alright and that it's them (Others) who are wrong. The first king of Israel, Saul, experienced this, and it drove him insane to a degree that he wanted to harm God's newly anointed, David.

As we know in the story, Saul still acted out the role of being king, but God had already chosen someone else. Saul still had the title of king before the people while God was building on David, a man after His own heart. This was having a form of godliness but being denied the power in its highest form (2 Tim.3:5). At this point of the lesson study, I would like us to keep in mind that I suggest that we keep an open mind like a window with an imaginary screen to keep the flies out (False or Misconceptions). Also, we forget everything we thought we knew about God's Word (meaning putting it on the back burner) and unlearn it so we can learn, so to speak. In conclusion, Taking into consideration that the book of Revelations consists of signs and symbols that we can open to our disposal. It's coded, and we can and will decode it along spiritual guidelines.

. . .

I would like to encourage you to continue to keep an open mind like an open window and practice principles before personalities. And continue to ask The Holy Spirit what you can do to make a difference in what you've heard and learned. We will be turning the corner so-to-speak with the revelation knowledge at a deeper, broader evaluation, so let us remember to "Unlearn so we can learn," so to speak. Note: Gal. 4:16. Later today or tomorrow, we will go forth with this "Truth" that has stood afresh all this time but is taken lightly for whatever reason.

I hope and pray all is well and our minds are refreshed by proper rest and relaxation. As we continue to view the condition of the Church of Laodiceans spoken of in Revelations, let us keep in mind that we, as the Body of Christ, can identify with all facets of this church. This is so because history truly repeats itself, and there's nothing new under the sun. Satan has no new tricks or ways to manipulate us; it's just modified (Eccles. 1:9-11, 1 Corinth. 10:13). In Rev. 3:15, 16, the Lord says that the church was lukewarm, neither hot nor cold. And He wishes they were hot or cold. Once again spoken, a lukewarm condition invites compromise and imaginary lines such as grey areas. The straddling of the fence so-to-speak. This is where the sit of confusion lies, and one would be caught between two opinions. This is where unwanted pressure resides, leading to poor decision-making (1 Kings 18:21). This can lead to quick decisions instead of thinking about a matter all the way through with prayer and meditation.

Remember the five virgins who came up short! They were lukewarm, and when it was required of them to go that extra mile, they came up short. They had good intentions, but their good intentions didn't get them to the marriage supper to meet their bridegroom. This was a parable in which Jesus told about the conditions of those representing Christ. Five of them made it, but five of them came up short. They came close, but close only counts in horseshoes and hand grenades. 99 1/2 won't do! Those of us who are straddling or in a backsliding condition have a tendency to put too much focus on comparisons, which can prevent us from reaching our maximum potential in life. We compare ourselves with people who we think are a level or levels higher than us and use this as a mark of excellence as a goal to strive for. This can and will stunt our spiritual and secular growth. Let The Holy Spirit be our definition of vocal and visual points. Believe me, The Holy Spirit will give us a start and finish concerning this! I'm so glad that Jesus took time out to give us parables as a way to identify with things that may seem obscure. He taught in parables as visual aides and picture stories. This was to give us mental pictures of the things we use in everyday life, as well as behavior patterns and health issues.

Okay, the Lord said that He wishes that we were hot or cold, not lukewarm. Here's the reason: a person on fire for the Lord will follow through by being sensitive to the moves of God in our daily living, which will enable us to move from glory to glory! A person cold is at rock bottom, at their lowest of terms, back against the walls, which makes us a good candidate to now listen to the voice of God through people, places, and things. When one is flattened to the level of the ground, there's no better alternative but to look up! When our backs are against the wall, our solutions for ourselves are exhausted, and God's solution now is clearly seen and accepted when, in the past, we denied His way! Now, O, how bright the path! Here's a matter of things that are not too hot and not too cold. This caters to our sensitive levels, which can easily be controlled by our feelings and emotions, which can keep us from exercising faith, which overrides our five senses. There are those of us who can't hold anything in our stomachs that are lukewarm to a degree of vomiting. Beverages that are under certain temperatures make them sick to the stomach! This is what God was giving us to illustrate our conditions and what they mean to Him. Take Heed!

As we continue to move closer in this lesson study, let us keep in mind that God is able to take us higher in His will for our lives by yielding ourselves to commit to what we know to be true on a small scale. Meaning we can be disobedient in areas we know of and think to ignore it and want more from God. Our Father doesn't work like that! I pray that we don't quench or grieve the Holy Spirit, which is our source of moving higher and higher in the things of God. May we be careful to walk in all the truth we know in order to receive more of God's Truth. The Lord said that signs shall follow those of us who are in tune with The Holy Spirit. It is literally said in King James's version that signs and wonders shall follow those who believe. And if we believe, surely we're tuned in to The Spirit. (Mark 16:17). I said this to say that we're to do God's will, and the signs of doing his will will be accompanied as evidence. We aren't to lead off by looking and seeking signs to fulfill our quest as believers. Signs have their place in our walk with Christ, as we will see.

Signs give us directions from point "A" to"B".They give us leads in life to make the way clear. It's also important to know the meaning of symbols and signs, like when one is applying for a driver's license on a written test. And preparation is a rule of thumb to master un-wanted "What if." So, let's identify with some signs, symbols, and codes to help us understand God's message through "Revelations." Waters; Rev. 17:15, Ten horns; Rev. 17:16. We can see here that the ten horns represent nations or groups because no horns literally can hate someone as spoken of in verse 16. These horns represent The United Nations. It also says that the horns had hearts and minds as kingdoms who gave their positions (Kingdoms) to the beast v. 17. Woman; Rev. 17:18-.... great city which reigns over the kings of the earth. (The Vatican). Dragon; Rev.20:2-Satan; The Devil. A Thousand Years; Note: (2 Pet. 3:8). God's timetables are different from our rule. For example, The Word says one (believer) can set a thousand demons a flight whereas two can and will set 10 thousand a flight. Here, 1+1=10 instead of 2. I hope this explains itself. Clouds, Angels, Angels, Messengers such as us as humans.

Note, we'll see on occasions where Angels will describe literal angels as spirit beings. There will be occasions where more signs will need interpretation, and we will have to take God's Word for us and ask The Holy Spirit to help us agree. This is important for one to agree. (Amos 3:3).

Note: The bible from Genesis to Revelation is God's Authentic Word! The Old Testament points to the New Testament, and The New points back to the Old, giving us an account of Jesus' coming and preparing us for things to come in the new. We can cross reference from old to new and get a greater understanding of what God is saying. (Isaiah 28:10). Here's another interpretation of signs and symbols found in Matthew 17:1-3: Moses and Elijah appear. This is an indication, sign, and symbol that represents those who will be alive on earth when Jesus returns and those who will be in the grave when Jesus returns. Moses represents those of us who will be asleep, and Elijah represents those of us who don't see death. Note,

> "Death is just a sleep to those of us who are in Christ." (Rev. 14:13, 1 Thes. 5:10)

I'm excited to bring to the table this lesson study that's vital to our finishing as a Christian believer. You see, It's important that we get started (Accepting Jesus; The New Birth). The strong finish is most important because many who've started this journey have left "The Straight and Narrow" for whatever reason. Some because their health has gone from good to bad. Others because of the loss of relatives or close loved ones.

The most common lack of funds can cause us to question God in the struggle to keep our heads above water. These are the areas the enemy shoots our way to try and get us off "The Straight and Narrow." So, let's not give up or give in! Let's grow up and go over these mountains of adversity! We'll find out that God will give us all that we need to finish what He has started in us. Let Us use Romans 10:11-14 to jump-start us to launch out further into the deep. Daniel, just like John, was given this prophetic message, which is that we can bear a record of the things that have already come to pass. It's important to recognize that these two were people of prayer! They were in tune to recognize the voice of God. This is important because false prophets have crept into the church. Counterfeit Teachings have been passed down to give us a false conception of the things that pertain to holiness. Holiness is a character trait that we should enter into. It's our trademark, which one can be identified with. Ephes. 1:4, 5:27, 2 Tim. 1:9, 2 Pet. 3:11, Rev. 22:11). These scriptures let us know the importance of living holy from start to finish in what we say and do. Our diet can also be read here in Daniel 1:7, 8. Daniel and the three Hebrew boys were among the captives when Babylon invaded Jerusalem under the rule of King Nebuchadnezzar. Just like Saint John, Daniel was under the authority of the enemy (Their Oppressors), but the mission of God still went through.

CHAPTER 3
HEAD OF GOLD

Head of Gold; King Nebuchadnezzar - 1st. Kingdom, Babylon (Dan.2:38).

Chest and Arms - 2nd Empire ruled by King Darius (Mede), King Cyrus (Persia), (Dan.2:39,5:1,28-31) (Ram w/two horns) - Dan. 8:3,20.

3rd Kingdom - Belly and thighs-Bronze or brass (Greece); Alexander The Great (Dan. 2:39), Male Goat- Dan. 8:4-7,...suddenly a male goat came from the west, across the surface of the whole earth without touching the ground (Dan. 8:5) indicates that the goat was traveling at a great and high rate of speed.

4th Kingdom or Empire - Romans; Legs and toes, Iron/Clay (Dan. 7:7, 8, 11).

Also, 1st.Empire - Lion with eagle wings (Dan. 7:2-4).

2nd Empire - Bear with three ribs in its mouth (Dan. 7:5).

3rd Empire—Leopard with four heads and four wings (Dan. 7:6). Note: The leopard itself represents speed, but the wings represent record-breaking speed. The head represents the four generals who took over after Alexander The Great died, giving us a historical event of when Daniel was in the grave. I will explain more as we go along, Okay?

Revelations are our forecast of events that must come to pass. We will learn in what manner the stage is set for the anti-Christ, which is already at work on the earth according to the scriptures. (2 John 2:18-23). Anyone who denies Jesus's redemptive work on Calvary is considered an anti-Christ, according to scripture. (1 John 4:3).

Scriptures say it this way, (…) "and every spirit that doesn't confess that Jesus Christ has come in the flesh is not of God." "Spirit" here represents a living body or person. It goes on to say, "And this is the spirit of the Anti-Christ (K.J.V.). So, this lets us know that there's a spirit behind this mentality that can work in a person. Just like everything a person does, has a spirit influencing them. Please, let us understand that Satan is a counterfeiter, and this is how he gets his power. This is his greatest agent, "Counterfeit." Let us identify what counterfeiting means. "Counterfeit" looks almost identical to what's real in all areas, deceiving even the best of us. It masquerades or presents itself as that which is true and will try and manipulate the best of us. It would take someone who's an expert or professional to distinguish what is real or phony. I liked to use counterfeit money, for example, seeing that "Printing" was my vocational trade in high school, which helped me to come close to making phony money. I learned that there was a certain kind of green that made real money that wasn't at the public's disposal. One couldn't get that money green, and detecting it came quite easy because of the information my instructors gave me. This helped me know how to keep myself free from phony money.

There were a couple of more ways to identify the difference, which is that you will always see at least one inkling of an eyelash-like imprint on real money, and that's a fact, just to name one way. Without these heads up, I wouldn't be able to distinguish between the two. The Holy Spirit is the expert on detecting false or counterfeit religion with the help of our understanding of the bible. Paying attention to details minimizes the chances of being deceived. Fruit inspectors are we to determine a thing. (Luke 6:43-45). Satan has carbon-copied Jesus's moves in order to deceive whosoever. It's going to always take the anointing in order to defeat his antics. As we move forward in the next lesson, we will make a chart and call it Satan Vs Jesus, which I know will help us as we go further in our studies. There's more to learn in the scriptures in Revelations and Daniel that will lead us right up to the door, so to speak, when we allow the anointing to interpret the verses that we will study.

Memory Scriptures: (2 Cor. 13:5, 1 Thes. 5:21, 1 John 4:1)

The Great Controversy (Satan Vs. Jesus): Lucifer (Satan) envies Jesus, Yet he imitates Him and tries to steer us humans away from worshiping Him through "False Worship." The devil has set up a Counterfeit Religion which has been established since the First Martyr; The stoning of Stephen (Acts 6: 1-15, 7:2....Brethren and fathers listen...v.51...You stiff-necked and uncircumcised in heart and ears! (60, 8:14). Satan couldn't imprison and kill all the Christians in order to pressure them to renounce their faith (it backfired), so he joined the church (Can't Beat-em so Join them). He became a member and slowly but surely twisted the behavior of weak members who eventually detached themselves from the power source through The Holy Spirit and formed their own church (Religion; Man-made practices exercised in the church which makes them an "A Law Unto

Themselves) (A Cult). (Matt. 24:4, 5, 11-14, Rom.2:2-11, 1 Cor. 1:7-10, 4:5, 6:1-3).

Satan's main objective is to destroy the works of God, which is established through The Person of Jesus (Death, Burial, and Resurrection). We must be equipped to distinguish "True Worship" from false. (1 Cor.14:33, 2 Cor.6:14-18, 7:1, 11:13-15, 2 Thes. 2:3-12, 2 Tim.2:19, 3:1-7, 4:5). Those who live outside of God's Will are "A Law Unto Themselves." They have a belief system (Personal) that may seem to be God Based on certain things that they have read in the bible. But, If it doesn't line up with what Jesus and The Apostles taught, it's the nature of The Anti-Christ (Heb.3:12-15, 5:12-14, 6:1-6, 1 Pet. 4:7-11, 15-19, 2 Pet.2:1-4, 1 John 4:1-6, 2 John 1:4-11, John 4:23).

CHAPTER 4
THE GREAT CONTROVERSY (SATAN VS CHRIST)

Examine the comparisons in order to see that Satan has imitated Jesus's character. #1 with Christ with #1 with Satan #1-#7.

Christ | Satan
1. Dan. 9:25, 10:13. | 1. Ephes. 2:2
2. Rev. 5:4,5 | 2. 1 Pet. 5:8
3. 1 Pet. 5:4, John 10:11, Heb.13:20 | 3. John 10:12,13, Matt.7:15
4. 2 Pet.3:2 | 4. 2 Pet. 2:1
5. 2 Cor. 6:16-18 | 5. John 12:31
6. Gal. 4:6,7 | 6. John 8: 44-47
7. Rev.19:11-16 | 7. Rev.6:2

Memory Scriptures: Amos 3:7, Rom. 10:14, 15, 2 Corinth. 4:3-6, Ps. 25:14, Dan.5:14.

The Lord majors in keeping us updated with what He's doing and going to do. The scriptures give us accounts of a

God that gives us the breast of the facts in order to cater to His message of deliverance. To stay open and sensitive to be used by Him. The scriptures posted above let us know that God is in our favor, and His endeavors are to keep what He wants us to share clear and plain in order to keep us free from false worship. Let us not be named as those considered dogs and swine who think little of God's Word, which is precious and valuable for staying alive spiritually. (Matt.7:6).

Daniel saw an image that depicted kingdoms that were presently making history in his day and time. King Nebuchadnezzar, The Babylonian king, got a readout of his position and the part that he played in the making of history. Before it was all said and done, he ordered the whole kingdom to worship Daniel's God, who is "The True and Living God." (Dan. 2:46-49, 3:28-30, 4:34-37). This shows that one or a few can make a difference, which is a whole lot and enough in the things of God. But, After the king's death, his son dishonored him and went back to serving the gods of Babylon with all its practices that didn't give glory to "The True and Living God." The position of the image moved its way to the chest and the arms of silver ruled by the Medes and the Persians, who didn't spare anyone of Babylonian descent. None except God's Candles, The Hebrew Nation. Daniel and the Hebrew Boys' position was still held in high esteem within this empire as well. Once again, This depicts the nature of an all-mighty God who will deliver! He always leaves a remnant, remaining a small percentage to carry on.

God sends us out as sheep among wolves and wolves in sheep's clothing. But, not without power, which means strength and authority to defeat the works of the devil, which can look so much like that which represents Christ-Likeness.We, as His Anointed, can distinguish between what's real and what's false! (John 10:1-16, Matt. 7:13-23). A lot is said in these few scriptures about the very nature of those who twist the living word, which can have a deadly effect on its hearers. Please take time to examine them further before we continue.

King Nebuchadnezzar, Head of Gold (1st.Empire-Babylonia), before his death, acknowledged Jehovah, The True and Living God. (Dan. 2:46-49, 3:26-30, 4:34-37).

Next, King Darius and King Cyrus-Medes and Persia;2nd.Empire acknowledged The True and Living God of Daniel. (Dan. 6:19-28). The 3rd. Empire is none other than Alexander the Great, who was the belly and thighs of Greece. (Dan. 2:32, 7:6). In Daniel Chp. 7:6, we have a descriptive look at what is best described as a leopard, which by itself represents a high rate of speed; fast. The wings rep. Record-breaking speed. History has it that Alexander the Great conquered the world at such a high rate of speed and young age that he got idle. He drank himself to death and was buried in a transparent coffin filled with honey. After this, His four generals took over the kingdom. This is indicated by the four heads that were on the leopard. Here's another proven fact that God is an awesome God and on time, giving us always the breast of the facts. He cares about the shaping of things pertaining to holiness. Why? Because holiness is His character! It's His trademark. It best describes Him. This is how we can determine true worship from false. Please Believe there are a lot of traditions in the church that many have set up as holy, which is far from the character of God, which we will see as we move on through this valuable lesson study.

The 4th Empire we will see is made up of bits and pieces of a character of things we can identify with. The 4th. Empire is described as none other than the Roman Empire, which made its debut early in history and was present throughout

Jesus's time on earth. They rendered their taxes to Caesar, who was a Roman authority figure. (Matt. 22:17-21). Nero was an emperor of Rome, which Paul had to face. (2 Tim.).The Roman Empire's influences have reached from Jesus's time to the present day, which will be revealed later. Daniel gives witness to it as the legs of iron and feet of iron and clay. (Dan. 2:33, 40-43). These things were told to come to pass to later see the coming of the Lord after The True Church influences the world. (Dan. 2:44, 45). Let Us describe this 4th. Kingdom further. It was determined in an earlier study that the breaking down of the precious metals symbolized the weakening of the power structures.

Nevertheless, the Roman government proposed a mighty scare to Daniel, saying that it was the fearsome and powerful animal seen in his vision. (Dan. 7:7). It devoured and broke into pieces the residue, which means influence, power, and authority, in comparison to authority figures in that day and time. Residue rep.the groups that were leftover in that remaining of the time period.The ten horns rep. The United Nations has this power structure and has its influence on the horns mentioned. This 4th kingdom had human eyes, which indicates it thought like a human (Without the influence of godliness) speaking or bragging, which truly isn't the nature of The True and Living God....mouth speaking pompous words (verse 8 of Dan.7th chp.) (James 1:911, Rom.12:16).

(...) **A**nd there was another horn, a little one, coming up among them. Dan. 7:8.

The power of the little horn has been determined as of The Roman Empire, which is narrowed down to the pope. And without going into great detail, history has it, as foretold in the book of Daniel, the exact actions spoken concerning the wound that one of the popes suffered in order to usher in another one. The preciseness is laid before us, plain and simple. On a personal level, When I first got introduced to this prophetic message (back in 1985 as a part of my schooling), there were grafts and figures that added up and became well with my soul. God's Stamp of Approval was on the things that I learned. The Holy Spirit has led me in this direction to share along these lines first to explain the exact preciseness later. I've learned over the years a way to keep it simpler to not convey in such a way as to fall into a category as "A Certain Doctrine of a Certain Denomination." It will be revealed in a greater light as we continue; trust God! Things that are considered small or little have a tendency to want to carry a big stick, so to speak, in what they say and do. The Little Syndrome carries a complex and a need to be heard as one who has the power.

Seeking the attention of everything on site in order to later influence its surroundings. The main objective is to control everything on site to make up for a self-lack of some sort. The reverse psychology is that one small minority that's so-called in control or of power couldn't oppose much of a threat; it could be overthrown if it were to get out of hand. The concept is to win the votes of those considered "Big-wigs" on their team in order to bring others in or on. How many times have we allowed little things to go by without tidying up on them, and before you know it's out of hand? Then, A little becomes a lot on a negative note. The Bible says that it's the little foxes that spoil the vine. (Songs of Solomon 2:15).

Let us pause for a minute. I can't wait to go further and tie in The Book of Revelations in a greater light. We've been considering The Book of Daniel more because of its more details, but we will see the parallel of the two as we go along.

. . .

Memory Scriptures: Daniel 9:1-7, 1 John 5:1-3, 3:18-24. There's much said in these passages that set the stage for how important God's Covenant was established on Mt. Sinai. The Covenant overall lets us know two things that are inevitable. We should be willing to die for the covenant that identifies us to Jehovah in His likeness. Or we will die for not keeping the covenant because of the separation from Jehovah. There's more to be said and taught about the covenant, which can increase our level of confidence, which I'll share as we go along. But, one thing to know about the covenant is that God's Best is ours because He states, "What's Mine Is Yours." Jas. 1:17, 18. The Covenant is us stepping down from our rule ship in our lives (On the throne or our hearts) and making a decision to give our will over to the care of God. We're saying, "Lord, take my life in full. I've made a mess of it, and I trust you to be my wheel from here on! This attitude, first and foremost, before we do anything, will bring God on the scene in our lives through the person of Jesus. 2 Chron. 7:14, 15. The enemy works hard at keeping those of us from keeping this mindset because he knows it's what keeps God in the driver's seat. Rev. 12:17. Dragon: Satan, The devil. Rev. 12:9. The woman; The True Church.

Rev. 12:17.....and went to make war with the remnant of her seed (K.J.V.). The word "remnant" is a word that brings to mind sowing and using patterns. We use patterns of many sorts that are cut out to make what we desire. And that material that's not used after cutting out or the desired amount is what is called the remnant. The remnant is what's left of the original pattern—that which remains or is leftover. So, in short, the devil was wroth, Furious or very angry with the body of believers who were around at the last or closing of this earth's history. Those who were on fire for the Lord were speaking the truth in love at any cost. Those of us who weren't lukewarm symbolize those in the church who will fold under pressure. Those who bear the resemblance of the tare. Matt. 13:37-43.

...**F**our great beasts came up from the sea, each different from the other. Dan. 7:3.

Sea; Waters- Rev. 17:15......The waters which you saw where the harlot sits are people, multitudes, nations, and tongues. Dan. 7:15, I Daniel was grieved in my spirit within my body(We're spirits, and we possess a soul and live in a body; Our earthly suit), and the visions of my head troubled me.16th v. I came near to one of those who stood by and asked him the truth of all this. So he told me and helped me understand the interpretation of these things: v. 17 Those great beasts which are four are four kings which arise out of the earth.19th verse: Then I wished to know the truth about the fourth beast which was different from all the others, exceedingly dreadful, with teeth of iron and its nails of bronze, which devoured, broke in pieces, and trampled the residue with its feet,20th verse, and the ten horns that were on its head and other horn which came up, before which three fell, namely, that horn which had eyes and a mouth which spoke pompous words, whose appearance was greater than his fellows. This fourth kingdom had all the right things to say to win the votes of many. It was eloquent in speech. Smooth like fine oil. (Prov.5:3-5,). Its appearance captivated a live audience, so to speak, and got the attention of all who looked upon it. (Gen. 3:6, Ezek. 28:12, 13).

21st. verse- I was watching, and the same horn was making war with the saints, and they prevailed against them. 22nd.Until the Ancient of Days came, and judgment was made in favor of the saints of the Most High, and the time came for the saints to possess the kingdom. In the fullness of time, an outward showing will be that God's Church will reign openly. The Lord is doing a mighty work under-ground, speaking at a slow but steady pace because He wants all of us to come to a place of repentance. "Hell" is only reserved for the backsliding angels who rebelled at the beginning and Lucifer, who became Satan. (Dan. 7:15-22 compare Rev. 17:9-14).

Dan. 7:23.....The fourth beast shall be a fourth kingdom on earth which shall be different from all other kingdoms, and shall devour the whole earth.25th verse-He shall speak pompous words against the Most High, shall persecute the saints of the Most High, and shall intend to change times and law. Some translations say, "Think to change times and law." This simply means that the changing of things that this 4th power proposes won't influence The True Church. The change is already in effect as we speak, but there are those of us who haven't bit the fruit of its poison by knowing the truth. We know that God is the same today, tomorrow, and forever, and His Will is perpetual. And He's against anything that tries to change His System. (Matt. 5:17-20, Rev.22:18, 19). We read the 4th power devouring the saints, which is a terrible thing for any and everyone who does so because God will eventually cut them to treads! (Ps. 105:12-15).

Revelation is a book that gives us history, current affairs, and a printout of things to come. There are prophetic numbers that give us a precise account that comes close to letting us know the season in order to line up. But, as Jesus says in The Gospels, He doesn't even know the time of that hour. (Matt. 24:36). The conditions will be like doing Noah's Days, where the people of Noah's time didn't put stock in what he was saying because, overall, they were trying to figure things out with head knowledge instead of their gut feelings. I say this because, on a simple note, Noah was building a large boat far from the water on dry land, which I know caused them to think Noah was off his rocker. And to see how long of a time he preached not to see his message unfold allowed them to doubt. But God is not slack concerning His promise to us. (2 Pet.3:8-13)

One thing that stuck out the most to me in the story of Noah is the very fact that under pressure, he stayed focused and even though no one heeded God's Calling through him, he got his family together to meet the turning of a whole new world ushered in by the cleansing of water. The three most used tools of Satan were in full effect: Lust of the flesh, Lust of the eye, and the pride of life. (1 Jo.2:16, 17). People were too busy filling their pleasures and what seemed healthy in human life, bonding through the institution of marriage. (Matt. 24:37-39). The New Testament is full of conditions that add up to the coming of our Lord and Savior.

Also, The manner in which The Anti-Christ is setting up camp and what their angle is. (1 Jo. 2:18-21). Through these few passages of scriptures, we can see the importance of the anointing in order to stay with the whole truth and nothing but the truth. This is best described as The Spirit of Prophecy. (1 Jo. 2:20, 21, Compare-Rev. 19:9, 10, 1:9). I propose a few questions, which are also found in the bible study I've shared with many on Revelations in the past. There are two reasons why St. John was exiled to the island of Patmos; what are they? (Rev.1:9, K.J.V.).What is the testimony of Jesus Christ? (Rev.19:10). We'll explore more shortly.

. . .

The scriptures clearly let us know that the spirit of the Anti-Christ is derived from those of us who are considered the church. (I John 2:18, 19). Verse 19 lets us know the importance of continuing, keeping, steadily, etc., in the things that make for holiness and sound doctrine. (2 Tim.3; 16, 17).

The Bible says, "If we continue in His Word and Love which is the only truth, then we are his disciples indeed" (K.J.V. Jo. 8:31, 32). A strong finish is of high importance! To not fall by the way because of the cares of the world or persecution. (Mark 4:13-20). Satan is the author of rebellion because he rebelled in the beginning. He caused a strike or union uproar speaking in heaven. His argument was that God was unfair to make them (The angelic host) spiritual beings who could only give homage to Him. Creating them like robots, not being able to choose whether or not they wanted to be on God's team. Lucifer petitioned and got 1/3 of the angelic host to side with him, and this got them kicked out of heaven before God even made the world.

The very nature of God is to give us space to repent, which is what God presented to those who were rebelling. But Pride wouldn't allow the devil the satisfaction of denouncing his act of rebelling. So, Heaven was no longer their home or dwelling place. Pride was the first sin committed, and this was done in heaven by none other than Lucifer, who became Satan, The devil who deceives the whole world. This act of rebellion was found in Judas, who betrayed Jesus with a kiss. Eli's sons perverted the church and later suffered the consequences along with Eli, their father because he didn't stop them from doing their dirt. The people in that day and time disliked the church because of Eli's sons. This is a prime example that lets us know the effect one or two members can have on the actions of many. (1 Sam. 2:22-25, 3:11-17, 4:10-22).

These matters couldn't be stopped because those who rebelled were too far gone, which labeled them "Those of Perdition." We can get so far gone to be given over to be considered reprobate. (Rom. 1:28-32). They are always learning but not able to make anything out of what they so-called study. Speaking against the truth. (2 Pet. 2:1-3). Speaking evil of things they don't understand. (2 Pet. 2:12).

The message to the Church of Laodiceans was one of addressing their condition of being lukewarm (not hot or cold). They were guilty of "Pride" in one sense that blinded their nakedness, which was in the closet, so to speak. Their wealth and worldly accomplishments pacified them in the area of their misery. Their success in the eyes of the public kept them from seeing their deficiency in the spiritual department. They were like the person in the parable who climbed the corporate ladder to get rich and lost out because God required him to step over to the other side when he wasn't ready. (Lk. 12:16-20). Putting money first means loving it more than God, which will bring quick destruction. (1 Tim. 6:10-12, Matt. 6:24). They were spiritually bankrupt in the things of God and were blinded by their own corruption that cunningly led them astray. This is the prediction of God's Church, but it's not too late to heed the calling of a loving father.

Through this message, God reaches out to us and bids us by saying, "I counsel you to buy me gold refined...Rev. 3:18. As a lawyer to a client, take my sound advice and buy of me gold refined. Be it known that God's Wisdom is worth its weight in gold and is more desired than precious rubies or priceless diamonds. Taking God's advice and applying His Wisdom, which is to truly live in full, carries us over to having a good name as well. (Prov. 2:1-5, 8:14, 18, 19, Eccle.

7:1). As we read on in this passage (Rev.3:18), God uses a prop or visual aid of precious metal being refined. In the early days, the method was to bring precious metals such as gold, silver, brass, iron, etc., to a state of high quality; one would use intense heat in stages that brought what was called dross (Impurities) to the very top to be scrapped off. Then, The refiner would apply a little more heat up a notch more to get the remaining impurities and repeat the process until all of the fake substances were out of the precious metal. God was saying that His system and way of life present us as pure and without flaws before Him, like refined precious metal just out of the fire. He uses the word "Buy" in reference to the fact that it's worth paying for, and we should know that the best things in life don't cost us anything but the lending of our time and effort. The cost is just to sacrifice our attention. God says here that this would cover the church's nakedness, misery, wretchedness, and blindness by focusing on His Method. The Lord is reaching out to us to heal our backsliding, as spoken here in the scriptures.

CHAPTER 5
HOW SATAN JOINED
THE CHURCH

Stephen was the first martyr to accept the death, burial, and resurrection of Christ our Lord. This was opposed by the scribes and Pharisees who thought Jesus was a blasphemer because He said that He and the Father were one. Jesus told them that if you've seen the Father, you've seen Him. Jesus went to the temple as a custom and opened up the book of Isaiah, which pointed to the long-awaited Messiah, Himself. This rattled the religious leaders to a degree to set out to kill Jesus. Jesus got away from their hands through the crowd as they plotted to throw Him off a cliff. Jesus exposed them, and they were offended because they loved their sins. Their sins were hidden from those that they thought were of low degree, but Jesus saw right through them. He came to His own, but his own didn't receive Him. They thought they were doing God a favor by silencing Jesus. His own killed Him at the hands of the Roman government.

Also, the Jews were disappointed because they were looking for the Messiah to take His right position over their oppressors, The Roman Empire. This was the same argument that got the first followers of Jesus captured and slaughtered in arenas. They were burned at the stake, pulled apart by wild horses, eaten by wild lions and tigers, and beheaded. This Satan thought it would keep others from following this Jesus, but it back-fired. The people in the stands saw that those who were facing death had something to look forward to more than their lives, which was eternal life in Jesus. So, They joined them in the middle of the arena to be saved. What was Satan to do next? He joined the church and waited til they lowered their standards that kept them in harmony with God. This caused separation from God in the person of Jesus, and they didn't even know it. This has been going on ever since, which has led to this particular study. We will bear witness to this change through the diluting of The Word.

CHAPTER 6
THE ROEAD THAT LEADS TO HEAVEN

For those who are in the Wichita area, let's call Wichita Falls heaven, and you live in Electra; those in the metroplex, let's call Dallas heaven, and you live in Ft. Worth, and those in Huntsville call Houston heaven. Let's say I came by to pick you up at home to show you my brand-new 2014 Jaguar. I knew you knew the way to heaven, but I was new to the area and didn't know the surroundings.

Nevertheless, you had been around for quite some time and knew the route to get to heaven. I pulled up at your place and started blowing my horn, which was full of excitement. You eventually stick your head out the door and notice my brand new candy apple red Jag. I ask you to join me for a ride to Wichita, Dallas, or Houston to show me the way there, seeing that you knew how to get there perfectly. You tell me to give you enough time to get dressed properly so I can join you on the trip of a lifetime. You come out to get in the car, and I pulled from the curb, going towards 287, 30, or 46. When I get there, I go north on 287 to get to Wichita Falls instead of South on 287, west on 30 to get to Dallas instead of east on 30, or north 46 to Houston instead of south on 46. You immediately begin to talk to God in prayer to find a way to relay to me in such a way as not to offend me by using suggestive reasoning. You notice that my facial expression shows I'm excited, which can lead to you easily conveying this to me. You tell me that there's a good chance that we're going in the wrong direction because, to your understanding, heaven is in the other direction. I proceeded to say that I didn't think so because, along the way, I saw some signs that indicated differently based on what I heard others say about how to get to heaven.

You ask me if I am sure, and I say definitely! You begin to pray to the Lord again and let him know that you needed him to show up right then and there because this not only involved me as a lost soul but also you as a believer who knows better! The Lord gives you an inspired ideal that you're waiting for the right moment to execute. You begin to notice that the little details that I once was going on have been exhausted, and it shows on my face.

You asked me if we were going in the right direction, and I told you just to sit back and relax because I knew where I was going. I went on to say that my great, great, grandparents, grandparents, and parents took this route to get to heaven. You then began to suggest as we went down the highway to take the next exit to a service station to ask someone there for directions. I agree with this, and we will take the very next exit to pull up at the full-service spot at the gas station. The tenant comes out and asks if he could help us, and we ask him how to get to heaven. He then points us in the opposite direction to get to our destination. I tell the man to thank you rudely because I think that he doesn't know what he's talking about. Before I could get back on the freeway, you encouraged me to let you go into the service station to purchase a road map so that we could be sure. I agree that this would solve the matter immediately. You go in and come back out with the map, and to my discovery, I see that we were going in the wrong direction. I'm thankful for you and God, who didn't give up on me and led me to repentance.

In conclusion, the bible is the road map to get us and keep us on the right path. And many of us as Christians are on the right road but going in the wrong direction. Let us watch and pray (Lk. 21:36). This is the whole reason why this lesson study is so important. The enemy wants us to be subject to his mark and way of worship. Revelations, in their entirety, will expose the devil's ploy for us to understand and pass on.

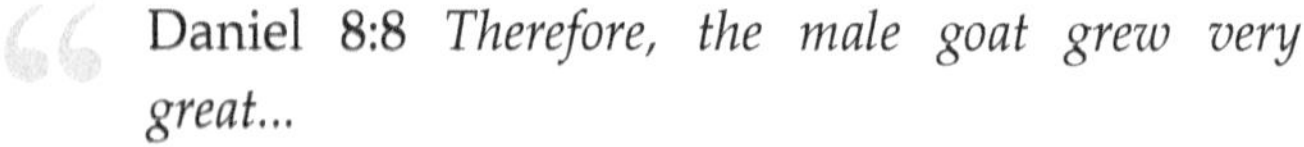

Daniel 8:8 *Therefore, the male goat grew very great...*

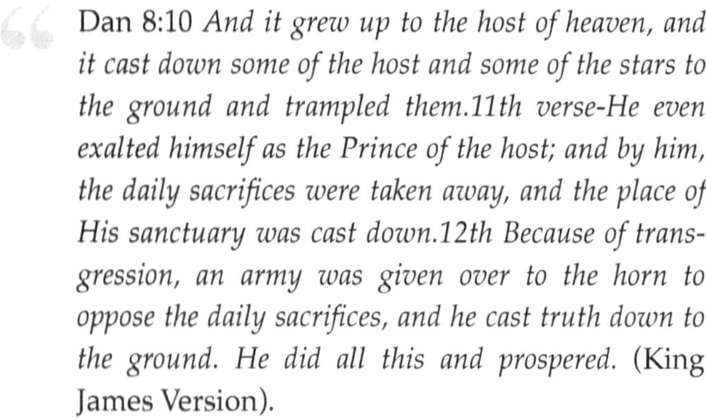

Dan 8:10 *And it grew up to the host of heaven, and it cast down some of the host and some of the stars to the ground and trampled them.11th verse-He even exalted himself as the Prince of the host; and by him, the daily sacrifices were taken away, and the place of His sanctuary was cast down.12th Because of transgression, an army was given over to the horn to oppose the daily sacrifices, and he cast truth down to the ground. He did all this and prospered.* (King James Version).

We see here that this power structure (The male goat) was high-minded and was and is a law unto itself. His mindset or ego grew the size of a God-like complex, which got the attention and votes of some very major forces in high places. This allowed his influence to spread like wildfire, and the power struggle began. Its organization begins to masquerade as "The True Power Source to Life," which is Jehovah, The True and Living God. There was no more room for them when they went from allied to anti. It imitated Jesus Christ, the Prince of Peace, which led many astray and formed an army of degenerates. It became a spiritual war, Satan Vs. Christ. Satan joined the church, so to speak, to later form his own church that transgressed or separated itself from the truth. It had a form of God but denied The True Church and all it stood for.

(2 Tim. 3:1-5). This is the very nature of Lucifer, King of Tyre, King Nebuchadnezzar, and Samson, just to name a few. You may say, "How did Samson make the list"? Well, Let's look at Samson in a different light. Samson knew who he was in God, which brought out the wrong side of him. He knew he was chosen by God with an edge because of his strength. He didn't take advice from his parents and dated outside those who didn't respect the attributes of God. This opposed everything that God stood for. He embraced the women of their arch-enemies and rubbed it in their faces. He picked fights in which he knew he would win. He embraced revenge like it was a part of his body. His actions got his wife's family killed to lose everything they own. Samson was a man who had haughty eyes and a temper to go along with it. His cockiness got his eyes burnt out, but God made use of Him in the end. Samson's decisions cost him his life! But, God, being the God that He is all by Himself, used Samson still at his lowest point. Truly, All things work together for God's Purpose. (Rom. 8:28)

We've already studied to get to the heart of the matter, to forever place principles before personality. We will learn of the great deceptions that the world, as well as the saints, have embraced, who have set up a belief system that will crash and burn at a time that I hope and pray is right here and now and not on Judgement Day when it's too late to denounce

---

Memory Texts: Proverbs 14:12, 2 Thess. 2:9-12

God gives us just what we need to make it in society on every level. He's mindful of our situations based on the decisions we make. Our choices make the things of God easy or complex. It's laid out for us so simply that it's looked over or passed off as needing to be improved. It's the simplicity of the gospel by mere obedience that keeps us understanding. You can best believe most of the time when we don't understand the things of God, even in daily living, because of disobedience. Somewhere, we didn't yield to that small, still voice inside of us that speaks to our spirit, man. Paul said that when he purposed to do the right thing, evil was all around, influencing his bad side to do what he knew wasn't of God. He said he recognized another law in him (The Law of Sin) working against him, bringing out the worst in him. He would use his liberty of choice to feed his sinful nature that opposes everything that God stands for (Rom. 7:14-25). We are free moral agents, which means we can choose to do right or wrong.

We must be careful not to get in the habit of doing wrong (Rebelling; Quenching The Spirit) because this releases a power or force that automatically numbs us to The Will of God. The Father's Hands become tied, and by law, it releases us over to perdition (Rom. 1:24,....who exchanged the truth of God for a lie v. 25-28). We exchange God's Truth for a lie when we live a lie after knowing His Truth! And to know the truth and not walk in it is a "Sin." And what is "Sin," Lawlessness (1 Jo. 3:4-8). We are to get in the habit or exercise of doing God's Will. And we can't do it without Jesus and The Holy Spirit. We can't clean up enough for God outside of pleading the blood, which simply means recognizing our limitations and having an attitude by saying, Lord, I can't do it alone; give me the ability to go through on a daily basis.

D an. 8:12....and he cast truth down to the ground.

This means that it didn't live by or stand for the truth. Its actions were one of rebellion. A law unto itself. Detached to God's Character or Image. This is important for us to understand because an act of rejection of God's Law is to be considered "Pride" and Blasphemy. Blasphemy is to pledge an alliance to another power source outside of God. It's to have a God-like complex and form groups that give homage to a calling outside of God's Will. This government or power structure spoken of here in Daniel gave no regard to God's Nature and led parties and worldwide groups in the rebellion against God. Dan. 7:25 He shall speak pompous words against the Most High and intend to change times and laws. How well do we know, and to what degree, that this group or entity has already made its mark? Let's name a few. On God's Time Table, it's 360 days in a year. Man, The Beast says it's 365 or added five more days. And has given us what they call "Daylight Saving Time." The man tells times or marks time by midnight or 12 o'clock, but God" 's telling of time is from sunset to sunset or evening to evening.

A new day is ushered in or first said to be a different day when it gets dark. This makes a big difference in the things of God, which we will see as we go on. Man wants to make an attempt to simplify things, but instead, he complicates things, causing confusion. And God is not the author of confusion! Man, from the beginning, thought he was doing God a favor and tried to build a tower high to the heavens in an act to be like God. God scrambled things to stop this movement of one world order. He Babel the situation, which means "Confused about the situation."Babel" means "Confusion." This is where the word "Babylon" is derived from."Babel" is the root word. John in Revelations compels us to come out of Babylon because it has fallen! Come out of confusion in another sense (Rev. 14:8, 18:2, 4, 5). This same beast spoken of here in Daniel is the same one in Revelations 13:3-8.

R ev. 13:1, Then I stood on the sand of the sea. And I saw a beast rising up out of the sea. He has seven heads and ten horns, and on his horns, he has ten crowns, and on his heads, he has a blasphemous name.

v.2....The dragon gave him his power, his throne, and great authority.

Rev. 17:15....The waters which you saw where the harlot sits are people, multitudes, nations, and tongues.

v. 16, And the ten horns which you saw on the beast, these will hate the harlot,....

v. 17, For God has put it into their hearts to fulfill His purpose, to be one mind, and give their kingdom to the beast,.....

v. 18, And the woman whom you saw is that great city which reigns over the kings of the earth.

We see here that this beast was crowned ten times, which means that it won the votes of the multitude as a whole. It got its power from the dragon or the work of the devil. Just like the devil when he was Lucifer in heaven, he became haughty, high-minded, and proudly lifted himself up to portray the role of "The Most High" God, which is "Blasphemy"...and on his head a blasphemous name. There's a name that is penetrating or circulating in the religious circle, and that word is "Vicar."This word means God's Active Force or Agent on earth. This is none other than The Holy Spirit. This has been and will always be from the beginning to the end. (Gen. 1:2, John 14:26, 16:7, 8). However, there are physical human beings who think of taking this title in their own way or style of worship.

A vicar is a representative, deputy or substitute; anyone acting "in the person of" or agent for a superior (compare "vicarious" in the sense of "at second hand").
Vicar (Anglicanism) - Vicar of Christ - Vicar general - The Vicar of Wakefield
(Latin vicarius, from vice, "instead of")
In canon law, the representative of a person clothed with ordinary ecclesiastical jurisdiction. The office of vicar was in use among the ancient Romans (Latin vicarius, from vice, "instead of")
In canon law, the representative of a person clothed with ordinary ecclesiastical jurisdiction. The office of vicar was in use among the ancient Romans,
*Vicarius Filii Dei (Latin: Vicar or Representative of the Son of God) is a phrase first used in the forged medieval Donation of Constantine to refer to Saint Peter, a leader of the Early Christian Church and regarded as the first Pope by the Catholic Church. Its interpretation has been disputed, at times, during the past four centuries. **

R ev. 22:14, Blessed are those who do His

*   n.wikipedia.org/wiki/Vicar

commandments that they may have the right to the tree of life and may enter through the gates into the city.

What gives us the right to enter the city and to survive off of the Tree of Life? Answer: Those who do the Father's commandments. This is also the key to being blessed and in the grace of God.

Rev. 20:6, Blessed and holy is he who has a part in the first resurrection. Over such, the second death has no power...and shall reign with Him a thousand years. V. 7, Now, when the thousand years have expired, Satan will be released from his prison.

So, we can see here that two resurrections will take place, and we do not want to be a part of the second one. Those who didn't accept the beast's mark or image are those who didn't worship it as well. They are those who will reign with Christ for a thousand years and forever more and who will be in the first resurrection, which is to eternal life, not death. (Rev. 20:4, 5).

Rev. 14:12, Here is the patience of the saints; here are those who keep the commandments of God and the faith of Jesus. We see here that keeping the commandments of God ties us in with faith in Jesus Christ. Just like our beliefs put into action, they go together to produce "Faith." Without these two components, "Faith" would not be possible! (Jas. 2:14-22). v. 13...Blessed are the dead who die in the Lord from now on. "Yes," says the Spirit, that they may rest from their labors, and their works follow them.

Luke 13:23, Then one said to Him, Lord, are there few who are saved? v. 24...Strive to enter through the narrow gate, for many, I say to you, will seek to enter and will not be able.

Matt. 22:14, For many are called, but few are chosen.

Please understand that God doesn't wish for any of us to perish or miss out on The New Heaven or Earth, but because of disobedience, many shall miss out. God's Law is His Character, and with that being said, He doesn't say one thing and do another. Let's take The Law of Gravity into account. What goes up must come down. God loves us with endless love. But, If we were to climb up on something high and jump off head first, God wouldn't dispatch angels to save us. This would be going against His Will or Law that's already set in motion. He won't change character! Many are called to the "Marriage Supper of the Lamb," meaning The Father extends the invitation through Jesus to all, but Many aren't accepting the invitation for whatever reason. If we accept "The Calling," we will be chosen!

I will be adding to this particular post through editing here shortly to continue on what has been started concerning "The State of the Dead" and where they go, which is highly important in giving us comfort in the scriptures concerning our loved ones who sleep in the dust. There's hope beyond the grave! Stay tuned, Derrick.

Note: There will be two classes of people on earth alive when Jesus Christ returns. Those who bear the " Seal of God," The Saved, and those who have "The Mark of the Beast, The Unsaved. Those who don't have The Seal of God will burn to a crisp as if the sun had moved up a little out of its place by the brightness of Jesus's Coming. (2 Thes.2:5-10).

Those of us who are saved will just blend in and float right up to heaven to reign with Him in heaven before it leaves its place in the sky. There will be two classes of people in the grave when Jesus cracks the sky with the sound that will awaken the saints in the grave only to join those who didn't see death when He comes. This will be one act. Those saved living and those saved that were in the grave will together levitate to the throne room of God, where we will go over "The Books" to assure us the reason why those who didn't make this final and only trip to be clarified as "Righteous Before God. " Note: There are two books. What are they, and what is their purpose? One- Bearing the records of all who lived on earth of what they said and did. The Lamb's Book of Life; to those of us who made it to reign with God in "The New Jerusalem. " (Rev. 20:12,15), John 14:1-3, 6, 25-28.

1 Cor. 15:20-27, 51-57. After the thousand-year reign, will the graves of the unsaved be open to stand before God, the Father, Jesus, Our Crimson Redeemer, The Angelic Host, and Us to be sentenced to "The Second Death"?

Note: There have been no human beings since the first death (Abel) in heaven looking down on us and viewing the activities on the earth! Our loved ones see the trouble we go through robbing them of their peace, which was granted unto them as a gift from God when they were laid to rest. This would be a grave injustice of the saying, "Rest in Peace." The body goes back to dust, and our spirit goes back to God, The Giver of Life. This doesn't mean that the person who has been laid to rest is conscious or aware. Read Eccles 9:5-10, 12:13, Let us hear the conclusion of the matter: Fear God and keep His commandments, For this is man's all. v.14, for God will bring every work into judgment, including every secret thing, whether good or evil. The scripture that says, "To be absent in the body is to be present with the Lord" is taken out of context. Our very breath goes back to God, who gave it to us. Our spirit is with God but not as a living being. These are the components that make up a living being: The breath of life, a body, a spirit, and a soul. These parts, in unison, make up a human being mind, body, and soul. But when one dies, his spirit separates from the body and loses its connection to a living being. The very first debate or argument brought up by Lucifer, saying that God was unjust, not giving the angels a choice in the matter of whether they wanted to worship him or not, an act of not being loving or fair, will be the same one in the end. But, the devil will be silenced in the end, which is at the judgment, when we will witness with Jesus and all in heaven, going over the books. This will determine why those who didn't make the first trip will be the first resurrection. We will see in the recordings presented by the recording angels the rejections of many who said no over and over when God sent laborers through His saints. This will close the accusation of Satan, making it seem that God isn't A Loving God of Second Chances. Read: Ezek. 9:1-11, 1 Pet.4:17.

Note: The scripture that states, "The dead in Christ shall rise first, "simply means first in comparison to those who were dead, not in Christ. This doesn't mean that those of our loved ones who have experienced death are already in heaven before us who are living! We'll all get there at the same time! But, we'll let preachers preach to our loved ones up in heaven. This is not of the scriptures spoken in the holy bible. This is man-made and one of the many deceptions that we will learn. Am I your enemy because I tell you the truth?

The devil masquerades as the true angel of light with the intent to deceive many. He's loose for now in the earth realm, but He'll be apprehended for a thousand years. Let's get to the events that lead up to his capture.

Rev. 20:1, Then I saw an angel coming down from heaven, having the key to the bottomless pit and a great chain in his hand. v.2, He laid hold of the dragon, that serpent of old, who is the Devil and Satan, and bound him for a thousand years; v. 3, and he cast him into the bottomless pit and shut him up, and set a seal on him so that he should deceive the nations no more till the thousand years were finished. But after these things, he must be released for a little while.

John best described what he saw that was given to him figuratively spoken and with signs and symbols. In the event that the saints (Dead or alive) are taken up to be with the Lord when Jesus returns (The first resurrection), those left on earth are the unsaved who accepted the mark of the beast. The unsaved dead are still in their graves to await their trial after the thousand years are up. The unsaved that were alive when Jesus came back to redeem those of us who are "His Seal" will be dead with their bodies scattered all over the world because they were burnt by the brightness of Jesus's Coming. They didn't have "The Seal of God" to absorb "The Light" to be a part of it (Jesus). So, The saints aren't on earth anymore, and the unsaved are dead in the grave and on top of the soil as well. Whose left?

The devil and his poses. His hands are tied! This means that there wasn't anyone left on earth to deceive anymore at that time. His hands are tied. Remember When you were young and coming up, and there was a time in your life when you hit a dead end on a matter? You were caught between a rock and a hard spot, so to speak. Your hands were considered tied up. Parents would use this saying with a rebellious child who they felt that they couldn't do anything with. Take this into consideration to sum up these verses. During the thousand-year reign, The saints will be partying and catching up on things with their loved ones who they've missed; unanswered questions will be addressed, and we will be enjoying our mansions and quality time with the Lord, just to name a few. Most importantly, we will witness the acts of those who didn't make it to the first resurrection and who had to wait until the thousand years were up. Their fate will be determined in the second resurrection, which is eternal damnation.

Memory Text: James 2:26- For as the body without the spirit is dead, so faith without works is dead also.

Luke 18:7, 8, And shall God not avenge His own elect who cry out day and night to Him though He bears long with them? v.8, I tell you that He will avenge them speedily. Nevertheless, when the Son of Man comes, will He really find faith on the earth?

1 Pet. 1:15, but as He who called you is holy, you also be holy in all conduct.

V.16, because it is written, "Be holy, for I am holy."

V. 22, Since you have purified your souls in obeying the truth through the Spirit....

Rev. 22:7, Behold, I am coming quickly! Blessed is he who keeps the words of the prophecy of this book.

Rev. 1:3, Blessed is he who reads and those who hear the words of this prophecy, and keep those things which are written in it; for the time is near.

We see here in Revelations, from the very first chapter to the very last chapter, encouragement coming from God, calling those of us who take to heart its message as "Blessed." May we continue observing this lesson study with an open mind and invite you to hear it in what might be different from what you're accustomed to hearing? Trust The Holy Spirit's ability to teach us by separating truth from error. Let's talk a little about "Judgment Day" in light of the messages of Saint John and Daniel and compare them with one another. John was allowed to look into the courtroom as the judgment was being set in motion: The Great White Throne Judgment. (Rev. 20:11-15). Notice that only those that were lost or unsaved were being judged. This is because those of us who are in Christ were already judged and accounted worthy, being witnesses of the unsaved in the courtroom.

Daniel gives an account of the judgment as it hadn't taken place yet. (Daniel 12:1-3). Can you just imagine those who aren't in that number or who didn't go up with Jesus in the first resurrection, waking up in the second resurrection thinking it was the 1st? One. They wake up out of the dust to be allowed the breath of life, to be judged and found guilty, and to be thrown in "The Lake of Fire"! This is tragic! Our past is important, with hopes of leading us onward in our Christian walk, but I pray that we will be found doing The Master's Good Bids at the end of this earth's history. Then, we can be ushered into The New Heaven and Earth. Let's keep our spiritual ears and eyes open and sharp.

Memory Text: Dan. 9:4.., "O Lord, great and awesome God, who keeps His covenant and mercy with those who love Him, and with those who keep His commandments,…"

John 14:15- "If you love Me, keep My commandments."

The word "If" implies a condition, meaning that if one does what is asked or is in their best interest, then the benefit or reward is automatically released. The next verse lets us know the reward or benefit of obeying The Command-ments. V.16, And I will pray the Father, and He will give you another Helper, that He may abide with you forever- V. 17- the Spirit of truth,...v. 26. But the Helper, the Holy Spirit, whom the Father will send in My name, He will teach you all things, and bring to your remembrance all things that I said to you. Dan. 8:12, Because of transgres-sion, an army was given over to the horn to oppose the daily sacrifices and cast truth down to the ground. He did all this and prospered. Here's a prime example of one getting by, but it won't get away. As we read the end of this prophecy, we see the vision Daniel was allowed to see. (Matt.16:26).

In the early parts of this lesson study, we learned that Daniel and his three companions (Shadrach, Meshach, and Abed-Nego) were allowed to pass the formula on to King Nebuchadnezzar. Daniel saw an image or statue that depicted kingdoms or empires that two of Daniel lived through and two that were the future for him. Daniel 2:34, You watched while a stone was cut out without hands, which struck the image on its feet of iron and clay, and broke them in pieces. V. 35,... And the stone that struck the image became a great mountain and filled the whole earth. Many are led to believe that this is none other than Jesus Christ, but as we read on, we can determine that it's "The Body of Christ," The True Church. This church was said not to be man-made but anointed and power-driven by The Holy Ghost. (....a stone was cut out without hands). Here are more passages that depict this Stone. Mountain, Church, Body of Believers.

Micah 4:1, Now it shall come to pass in the latter days that the mountain of the Lord's house shall be established on the top of the mountains, and shall be exalted above the hills. People shall flow to it. V. 2, Many nations shall come and say, "Come and let us go up to the mountain of the Lord, To the house of Jacob; He will teach us His ways, And we shall walk in His path." We can read here in the scriptures that "The Church of God" will be lifted or raised to a height that's above other mountains or so-called institutions resembling The True Church at this time.

John 12:32, "And I, if I am lifted up from the earth, will draw all peoples to Myself."

Zechariah 8:3-... Jerusalem shall be called the City of Truth, The Mountain of the Lord of hosts, The Holy Mountain. It's very important for us to strive to keep the pureness to be accounted as those who will go in and out teaching what The Spirit utters. Especially knowing that there are false teachings among us. Teachings mixed with a little bit of truth and a whole lot of error.

D aniel 7:23, "The fourth beast shall be A fourth kingdom on earth,"v.25, He shall speak pompous words against the Most High and intend to change times and law. Then the saints shall be given into his hand…

The words spoken by this authority figure will be against everything that God stands for, which is to compromise God's Way of Being. What is God's Way of Being? Holiness!

1 Pet. 1:15, but as He who called you is holy; you also be holy in all your conduct (K.J.V.)

....in all your conduct. This lets me know that living holy is a lifestyle that meets God's Approval. This is in what we say and do. Romans 12:1 lets us know that our bodies are to be given to holiness as if it was placed on the altar as a sacrifice. And we know that that which was presented on the altar was clean or pure before God in order to be given over as a sacrificial offering. That means We are to keep ourselves fit for the Master's Use, which is symbolically giving ourselves up as a burnt offering.

Rev. 22:11, Let us know the importance of being holy right down to the wire.

V. 11-.; "he who is holy, let him be holy still."

But, if one were to take away from God's Way of doing things, this would be to think to change God's Rule, which is unholy. This speaks against God's Provision to keep us holy, which is blasphemy. This is actions speaking out pompous words like the beast spoken of in Daniel 7:23.We are either for God or against Him. This has a form of godliness, which is spoken of in 2 Tim. 3:5. It goes on to say....but denies its power, which means "Godly Authority." This is establishing one's own rules and regulations outside of The Will of God. Denying God's Commandments, Laws, Precepts, Judgments, Testimonies, etc. And it goes on to say ..from such people turn away! This is the very nature of one making his own mark or statement. Matt. 7:21-23. We must work out our salvation as if it were life-threatening, which it is! Phil.2:12.

Revelations Pt. 7 can't.

Rev. 13:18- Here is wisdom. Let him who has understanding calculate the number of the beast, for it is the number of a man: His number is 666.

Romans 1:18- For the wrath of God is revealed from heaven against all ungodliness and unrighteousness of men, who suppress the truth in unrighteousness, V.22-Professing to be wise, they became fools,v. 23- and changed the glory of the incorruptible God into an image made like a corruptible man, birds and four-footed animals, and creeping things.

Verse 25- who exchanged the truth of God for the lie and worshiped and served the creature rather than the Creator, who is blessed forever, Amen.

What it all comes down to is who is on the Lord's side. We are either for Him or against Him. And if against Him makes us enemies of Christ who is The Expressed Image of Jehovah God. The devil is The Father of Lies and has lied from the beginning. (Gen.3:1-4). He twisted the scriptures by using what we know as he did in the garden. Mixing truth with error is trying to cause us as people to question things of

God, which is a no-brainer! That's why we must search the scriptures and make use of the Holy Spirit to test every spirit. The Lord is not the author of confusion. And please believe what we don't know can harm us. (Hosea 3:6). Satan wants us to believe that God is our problem and He has set us up for failure with His rules and regulations. (I John 5:3).

#1-Ephesians 4:5- one Lord, one faith, one baptism;v.6-one God and Father of all, who is above all, and through all, and in you all.
#2-Revelation 11:4- These are the two olive trees and the two lampstands standing before the God of the earth. (The Old/New Testament).
#3- The Father, Son, and The Holy Ghost
#4- The Four Gospels (Matthew, Mark, Luke, and John)

The Four Living Creatures before the Heavenly Throne depicts the four facets of the image of Jesus.

The Lion-King of the Jews; Lion of Judah, Eagle; Deity, Ox; Servant; Man; Became flesh and dwelt among us (John 1:14)

#5- The Five Wise Virgins (Matt.25:1-13)
#6- "6" is the number of man and his efforts. It's a number or symbol of incomplete.
#7- "7" is the number of God.Also, the number or sign of complete, perfect, finish. (Gen.2:1-3).

We can continue with the Seven Feast Days, and everything done in the Sevens was perfect and complete in God's Sight and Power.

This is to perk our attention on the importance of numbers and what they mean to God. Man has made his debut with his patterns to shape what he thinks is best for mankind, which has grieved The Holy Spirit and quenched Him. (1 Thess. 5:16-19). Man says it's 365 days. In a year, calling it daylight saving time, On God's Time Table, it's 360 days. On God's Table, it's from sunset to sunset, determining a complete day when man calculates it at midnight. Man has made his mark, stand, or convictions, thinking it to be of sacredness with his ego, Edging God Out. This is the very nature of Satan, The Devil who deceives the whole world. (Rev.12:9,13:14,2 John 1:7). Man's attitude is, "If it feels good, then do it! Get all you can while you can, then sit on the can."Man looks at it as "Big Sin/Little Sin, Big "I'm" and Little "You's," Me, Myself, and I." Man measures success by the contents of possessions and God the contents of the heart. Let us continue little by little to grasp the big picture.

I saiah 14:12, How you are fallen from heaven, O Lucifer, son of the morning!

Lucifer means son of the morning star.

Who made Satan? You may say God is the Creator of everything. I bid the differ. God created Lucifer, and he became Satan, the Devil when he rebelled in heaven. Verse 12 Asks a question about how Lucifer fell from from heaven. Next, How do you cut down to the ground? Verse 13 gives us the answer: For you have said in your heart: I will ascend into the heaven, I will exalt my throne above the stars of God; I will also sit on the mount of the congregation...Verse 14 goes on to say, I will ascend above the heights of the clouds; I will be like the Most High. Lucifer wasn't satisfied with being next or 2nd to God as the chief angel and director in heaven. He wanted all the glory and, for all the wrong reasons, a level of respect or reverence for The Most High God, Jehovah. This got him and 1/3 of the angels expelled from the very presence of God. Disobedience is "Sin," and sin is separation from God upon whosoever exercises it.

Rev.12:7-9, 9 gives us an account of what happened through what Saint John was allowed to see."Rebellion" is Satan's mark, which has written the story of many in the bible doing it their own way. It was the spirit of the Anti-Christ when Jesus came on the scene. Adam and Eve rebelled. (Gen.3:6). Cain killed Abel (Gen.4:8), John 8:44, Then, the lord saw that the wickedness of man was great in the earth and that every intent of the thoughts of his heart was only evil continually. (Gen.6:5). Verse 6, And the Lord was sorry that He had made man on the earth, and He was grieved in His heart. Then, Man got so full of himself to a degree that he wanted to build a skyscraper or tower straight up to the throne of God. So, God had to bring man back down to earth in his mind by confusing the language. Gen.11:4-9. The first king of Israel, Saul, got anxious and did the work of a priest or Samuel's profession, and the Spirit of the Lord left him. The anointing left his presence, and he literally lost his mind. 1 Sam. 13:7-14, 15:10-23. It's important that we do the Will of God and walk in all the truth we may know to be. We should allow ourselves to grow, which comes from being faithful in a few things, to grow and be counted on by God for greater missions. Obedience is truly better than sacrifices. This is because if we obey first, we won't have to sacrifice a prayer of forgiveness. We can move on with God in Jesus' name with the anointing going forth."Obedience" is one of God's marks or attributes. Let us stay tuned.

I trust that all that was said was inspired by The Holy Spirit, who guides us as instruments of the "Most High." We are at the highlight of this prophecy, which may seem like a lot of knowledge shared in spots leading up to a circle of unanswered questions. Well, Here's some news we can use based on what we may already know as mature people of God. All things work together for the good, giving us purpose in the things of God. Also, God's Character is flawless and best describes who He is and what His purpose is. Please Believe that God's Character is His Law. You can't separate the two. Example: Question-What is sin? (1 John 3:4)...for sin is the transgression of the law. To transgress is to break or violate. We know that "Sin" separates us from God. So, When we sin, we go against the nature or character of God, which is to break His Law. When we obey His Law, we obey Him plainly and simply. God's Character is "Love" as well. He so loved the people of the world that He gave His Only Begotten Son. (John 3:16). And we love Him because He first loved us. (1 John 4:19). We see here that the showing of love first from God compelled us to give love in return."Love" covers a multitude of sins as well. (1 Pet.4:8). This means that if we care for our fellowman, which is showing love, we won't do anything ill will towards them and if we do one towards another, we would be quick to forgive."Love" is what seals the deal so-to-speak. Without it, all our efforts to show who we are in Christ come to a big fat zero! (1 Corth. 13th Chp.). Let's keep it simple now! Jesus says if we love Him, we Keep His Commandments. (John 14:15). Also, This is a sure way to know that we love the Lord. (1 John 5:2) By this, we know that we love the children of God when we love God and keep His Commandments. And His Commandments aren't hard to live by or complicated to follow if "Love" is the contributing factor! (1 John 5:3). It brings us joy to do His Good Pleasures! (Ps. 112:1).

God chastens us, showing His Love as well! Meaning He uses "The Rod of Correction on us when needed. We may get by, but We won't get away with wickedness! (Heb.12:6). So, let us not get twisted about what and how God disciplines us. His wrath or anger will be without mercy in the "Last Hour" because we should have gotten it right by then. God always sends warnings before judgment. In the message to us by the three angels, we can see that those who received the mark of the beast and worshiped him drank the wine of the wrath of God, which was poured out without mixture. (Rev.14:10),…wrath of God, which is poured out full strength. Some translations read, "Without measure or mixture". This means that symbolically, mercy was taken out. Jesus, at this point, has taken off His priestly garments (Interceding for us) and put on His clothes to be ready to make war and judgment at His Second Advent. Woe unto those of us who don't have The Seal of God!Because those who don't are those who have received the mark of the beast in their foreheads! (Rev.14:6-12). Before we go any further, we will focus on these verses (6-12) to get an understanding of it in order to close out!

Rev. 14:6, Then I saw another angel flying in the midst of heaven, having the everlasting gospel to preach to those who dwell on the earth-.....

CHAPTER 7
ANGEL-MESSENGER

Angel here refers to the messenger. One may say, "How do I know this to be true"? I propose a question: Who has God given the calling through the Person of Jesus to share the Gospel with whomever on earth? Matt. 28:19- Go therefore and make disciples of all the nations, baptizing them in the name of the Father and of the Son and Holy Spirit,20 teaching them to observe all things that I command you; and lo, I am with you always, even to the end of the age. Amen.

Matt.1 6:18- And I also say to you that you are Peter, and on this rock, I will build My church, and the gates of Hades shall not prevail against it. 19 And I will give you the keys of the kingdom of heaven, and whatsoever you bind on earth will be bound in heaven, and whatever you loose on earth will be loosed in heaven. Here, we see an established truth given to Peter based on his relationship with Jesus. This was based on the fact that he knew who Christ was beyond the surface level. It's Peter getting his breakthrough!

We, like Peter, When we get to a place in our walk with God through Jesus to know the power of God to move mountains, knowing that we can do all things through Christ who strengthens us, We're well on our way to convert others to Christ. This should answer the question of who is sharing the gospel spoken of in Revelations. A literal angel has been commissioned to share the message of Jesus (Which is The Everlasting Gospel) to preach to all on earth. Of course, God can use whoever He chooses. He used a donkey in the past, just to name one incident. But He uses converted people like you and I. In this angel's message or believer's message, They're compelling others to worship The True and Living God who made everything. This is as if there were those who worship another. Joshua compelled the people to choose. Joshua 24:14- Now, therefore, fear the Lord, serve Him in sincerity and in truth, and put away the gods which your fathers served........Serve the Lord! 15-.....But as for me and my house, we will serve the Lord. Elijah said to all the people, "How long will you falter between two opinions? If the Lord is God, follow Him; but if Baal, follow him.

1 Kings 18:21. Matt. 24:14 Let us know that after every soul has had a chance to accept or reject the gospel, the probation period will be exhausted. Then the end shall come!

Rev. 14:6- Then I saw another angel flying in the midst of heaven, having the everlasting gospel to preach to those who dwell on the earth.....

I pray that it's established in this passage of scripture that this angel seen by John was a messenger of God, which could mean anyone who was sold out to "The Great Commission." Matt. 28:18-20. This should be so because we know that God, through the person of Jesus, gave everyone, whether Jew or Gentile, the power and credentials to make disciples after Christ. John says this messenger was flying in the midst of heaven. It could be very well understood that this messenger was in The Spirit Realm. Being in the Spirit puts one in one accord with God in order to receive God. Many times in the bible, we hear of believers being caught up in the atmosphere of God, which leads them to the very presence of God. We receive divine intervention through fellowship, prayer, fasting, and meditation. This is when God can use us more effectively to do His good bidding. A trance that puts one in a position to experience an out-of-body experience. To be absent in the body is to be present with the Lord! Peter was caught in heaven (A Trance) and saw a curtain or blanket that stretched from heaven to earth. He saw all kinds of food to eat and was told to eat. At that time, he didn't quite fully know what it meant, but one thing that was an established truth was that all things or foods on that blanket weren't for him to eat. This helped him to rule out some things that weren't clear so that he could later get the full understanding.

God was confirming the new dispensation of non-Jewish people to be inducted into The Kingdom of God. He knew just what to do and went to Cornelius's house to convert his whole family. Act 10th Chp. Paul was caught up in the third heaven and received of God. (2 Cor. 12:1-6). Ananias received from God through a vision, laying hands on Saul of Tarsus (Paul) to regain his sight after the Damascus Road Experience. This is a prime example (Ananias) of someone who was used to God bearing no more record of doing anything else miraculous in the bible but Is among the famous in God's Eyes. He played a very small part in bringing forth a man (Paul) who literally wrote the whole New Testament, which was major! That's how God works, From the greatest to what may seem least!

Revelations 14:8-And another angel followed, saying, "Babylon is fallen, is fallen, that great city, because she has made all nations drink of the wine of the wrath of her fornication."

Babylon was a kingdom in ancient history that fell at the hands of the Medes and Persians, spoken of in the early part of this prophecy. But. It also represents any Religious groups that aren't of The True and Living God.

"Babylon" comes from the root word "Babel," which means "Confusion."

This messenger assures us that the stronghold of falsehood in the church had reached its toll on those who were established by its influence. What was done in the dark is exposed or torn down by truth, no longer masquerading as the way to salvation! The word "Fornication" lets us know that its influence allowed all the nation to indulge in affairs that were an abomination to God. I thought about changing the way of worship that gave God glory. We will see the distinct difference that separates True/False Worship. God's Stamp of Approval or Seal will be clearly seen and understood.

In closing, I would like to propose a question to sleep on. I'll start by saying this. Many believe that theirs many roads that lead straight up to the throne room of God. And it doesn't matter how you get there.

One group of believers says that their doctrine is the key or road that leads to heaven, and all other attempts will lead to destruction. They believe that they're the power team that channels The Holy Spirit. There are so many denominations. How can we know which one or how many of them are true? There are those of us who believe that God is Love and that whatever attempts we make to be a better person illustrate what we think is God's Love toward our fellowman, it is enough to get in. And that God will let all of us in with this mentality. If we just believe in Jesus, they say. I know for myself that to believe in Jesus will compel me to do something about my life and bear fruit. This means that it will show up in my prayer time, study time, when I share my money gifts, etc. We'll be working out our soul salvation with fear and tremble. Meaning means being on our grind for the Lord! So, With all these denominations claiming The Body of Christ, How do we know for sure?

Key: There's one thing that sticks out the most, and that ties us into The Mark or Image of Satan. This is, for the most part, under the umbrella of Christianity.

CHAPTER 8
CHURCH OF EPHESUS (REV.2:1)

Accusation: You had left your first love (v.4). How many of us can remember when we first got saved and when the love of God was shed abroad in our hearts, and nothing could separate us from Jesus? A team of wild horses couldn't even turn us back. We were all eyes and ears for the things of God for breakfast, lunch, and dinner. We had tasted and seen that the Lord was good, and it got sweeter and sweeter as the days went by. But, Somewhere along the way, we got off track through people, places, and things. The cares of the world enabled us to go astray. The lust of the eye, the lust of the world, and the pride of life choked or killed our witness to where we didn't put God first place in our diet of things. We started looking and acting like the world was unsaved, and people couldn't tell if we were saved or not. We became unfruitful, which killed our witnesses and our testimony.

This is how the devil joined the church by the lowering of our standards. We begin to compromise our convictions, and our light becomes diluted. We stopped taking a stand and fell for everything! This was the condition of the first church mentioned here, Ephesus. O, and how this depicts the condition of the church in these last days. Note: We are as strong as the weakest link! Acts of Repentance: Remember therefore from where you have fallen; Repent and do the first work (V.5). This implies that The Great Commission is the same (Matt.28:18-20). God is the same, and He doesn't change according to scriptures (Heb.13:8, Malachi 3:6). It's the Uncompromised Word of God we're to uphold to death.

Do us part! We can learn to step on toes like Jesus did without messing up the shine in order to uphold our integrity. The main objective of the enemy is to lead us to change The Word of God, and heaven forbids it! It must have God's Stamp of Approval on it, or it will suffer in the time of testing or judgment. Keep in mind that God has a special seal or trademark for us to get in. Without it, every-thing we've done with good intentions for the building of the kingdom of God will suffer. When Jesus comes back for us, this seal is all that He sees and is governed by. Keep in mind what we don't know will be of vital importance to us to make it through this time of testing. What you don't know can hurt you! (Hosea 4:6). This gospel will be preached to every living soul before the end comes according to scripture (Matt.24:14). This means that in the lives of every individual, we will have time to hear the gospel message that leads to repentance to either accept or reject it. Jesus will be at the door or is at the door! Many are in the valley of decision or at the crossroads where the enemy wants to keep us confused. But, The Mind of Christ will allow us to be over-comers. God is not the author of confusion!

Revelations don't. Pt.7

As we reflect on the condition of the 1st. Church mentioned (Church of Ephesus)in Revelation, We, as the Church of Christ, can identify with being in a backsliding condition. However it came to be, it's a feeling of being totally lost and eaten up with guilt! But let us be reminded that God is married to the backsliders, who were us at one time in the past. (Jeremiah 3:14)

Consequences: Rev.2:5 - I will come quickly and remove your lampstand from its place. There's nothing more horrifying than being in a backsliding condition where the anointing has left one! Immediately, our minds are so under attack that we are quick to believe a lie that we're alright and that it's them (Others) who are wrong. The 1st king of Israel, Saul, experienced this, and it drove him insane to a degree to want to harm God's newly anointed, David. As we know in the story, Saul still acted out the role of king, but God had already chosen someone else. Saul still had the title of king before the people while God was building on David, a man after His own heart. This was having a form of godliness but being denied the power in its highest form (2 Tim.3:5). At this point of the lesson study, I would like us to keep in mind that I suggest that we keep an open mind like a window with an imaginary screen to keep the flies out (False or Misconceptions). Also, Forgetting everything we thought we knew about God's Word (Meaning putting it on the back burner) and unlearning so we can learn, so to speak. In conclusion, Taking into consideration that the book of Revelations consists of signs and symbols that we can open to our disposal. It's coded, and we can and will decode it along spiritual guidelines.

As we continue to move closer in this lesson study, let us keep in mind that God is able to take us higher in His Will for our lives by yielding to what we know to be true on a small scale. This means that we can be disobedient in areas we know of, think to ignore them, and want more from God. Our Father doesn't work like that! I pray that we don't quench or grieve the Holy Spirit, which is our source of moving higher and higher in the things of God. May We be careful to walk in all the truth we know in order to receive more of God's Truth. The Lord said that signs shall follow those of us who are in tune with The Holy Spirit. It is literally said in King James's version that signs and wonders shall follow those who believe. And if we believe, surely we're tuned in to The Spirit. (Mark 16:17). I said this to say this: We're to do God's will, and the signs of doing his will will be accompanied by evidence. We aren't to lead off by looking and seeking signs to fulfill our quest as believers.

Signs have their place in our walk with Christ, as we will see. Signs give us directions from point "A" to"B".They give us leads in life to make the way clear. It's also important to know the meaning of symbols and signs, like when one is applying for a driver's license on a written test. Preparation is a rule of thumb to master un-wanted "What Ifs. "So. Let's identify with some signs, symbols, and codes to help us understand God's Message through"Revelations." Waters; Rev.17:15, Ten horns; Rev.17:16.We can see here that the ten horns represent nations or groups because no horns literally can hate someone, as spoken of in verse 16. These horns rep. The United Nations. It also says that the horns had hearts and minds as kingdoms who gave their positions (Kingdoms) to the beast v.17.Woman; Rev.17:18-....great city which reigns over the kings of the earth. (The Vatican). Dragon; Rev.20:2-Satan; The Devil. A Thousand Years; Note: (2 Pet.3:8). God's timetables are different from our rule. For example, The Word says, One (Believer) can set a thou. Demons a flight where two can and will set 10 thou. A flight. Here, 1+1 = 10 instead of 2. I hope this explains itself. Clouds, Angels, Angels; Messengers such as us as humans.

Note, We'll see on occasions where "Angels will describe literal angels as spirit beings. There will be occasions where more signs will need interpretation, and we will have to take God's Word for us and ask The Holy Spirit to help us agree.

This is important for one to agree. (Amos 3:3). Note: The bible from Genesis to Revelation is God's Authentic Word! The Old Testament points to the New Testament, and The New points back to the Old, giving us an account of Jesus' coming and preparing us for things to come in the new. We can cross reference from old to new and get a greater understanding of what God is saying. (Isaiah 28:10). Here's another interpretation of signs and symbols found in Matthew 17:1-3: Moses and Elijah appear. This is an indication, sign, and symbol that represents those who will be alive on earth when Jesus returns and those who will be in the grave when Jesus returns. Moses rep. Those of us who will be sleeping and Elijah rep. Those of us who don't see death. Note, "Death is just a sleep to those of us who are in Christ. (Rev.14:13,1 Thes .5:10). Let Us pause for now, and we'll get back to God's Word shortly.Thanks, In Advance, Derrick.

Revelations Pt.7 can't.

Head of Gold; King Nebuchadnezzar - 1st. Kingdom, Babylon (Dan.2:38).

Chest and Arms - 2nd Empire ruled by King Darius (Mede), King Cyrus (Persia) (Dan.2:39,5:1,28-31) (Ram w/two horns) - Dan.8:3,20

3rd Kingdom - Belly and thighs - Bronze or brass (Greece); Alexander The Great (Dan.2:39), Male Goat - Dan.8:4-7,...suddenly a male goat came from the west, across the surface of the whole earth without touching the ground (Dan.8:5) indicates that the goat was traveling at a great and high rate of speed.

4th Kingdom or Empire-Romans; Legs and toes, Iron/Clay (Dan.7:7,8,11).

Also, 1st.Empire - Lion with eagle's wings (Dan.7:2-4).

2nd Empire - Bear with three ribs in its mouth (Dan.7:5)

3rd Empire - Leopard with four heads and four wings (Dan.7:6) Note: The leopard itself rep. speed, but the wings rep. Record-breaking speed. The head rep. The four generals who took over after Alexander The Great died give us a historical event of when Daniel was in the grave. I will explain more as we go along, Okay?

The 4th Empire we will see is made up of bits and pieces of a character of things we can identify with. The 4th. Empire is described as none other than The Roman Empire, which made its debut early in history all throughout Jesus's time on earth. They rendered their taxes to Caesar, who was a Roman authority figure. (Matt. 22:17-21). Nero was an emperor of Rome, which Paul had to face. (2 Tim.).The Roman Empire's influences have reached from Jesus's time to the present day, which will be revealed later. Daniel gives witness to it as the legs of iron and feet of iron and clay. (Dan.2:33,40-43). These things were told to come to pass to later see the coming of the Lord after The True Church influences the world. (Dan.2:44,45). Let Us describe this 4th Kingdom further. It was determined in an earlier study that the breaking down of the precious metals symbolized the weakening of the power structures. Nevertheless, the Roman government proposed a mighty scare to Daniel, saying that it was the fearsome and powerful animal seen in his vision. (Dan.7:7). It devoured and broke into pieces the residue, which means influence, power, and authority, in comparison to authority figures in that day and time. Residue rep.the groups that were left in that remaining time period. The ten horns rep. The United Nations power structure had and has its influence on the horns mentioned. This 4th kingdom had human eyes, which indicates it thought like a human (Without the influence of godliness) speaking or bragging, which truly isn't the nature of The True and Living

God....mouth speaking pompous words(verse 8 of Dan.7th chp.) (James 1:911, Rom.12:16).

Revelations Pt. 7 can't.

......and there was another horn, a little one, coming up among them. Dan.7:8.

The power of the little horn has been determined as of The Roman Empire, which is narrowed down to the pope. And without going into great detail, history has it, as foretold in the book of Daniel, the exact actions spoken concerning the wound that one of the popes suffered in order to usher in another one. The preciseness is laid before us, plain and simple. On a personal level, when I first got introduced to this prophetic message (Back in 1985 as a part of my schooling), there were grafts and figures that added up and became well with my soul. God's Stamp of Approval was on the things that I learned. The Holy Spirit has led me in this direction to share along these lines first to later explain the exact preciseness.

I've learned over the years a way to keep it simpler to not convey in such a way as to fall into a category as "A Certain Doctrine of a Certain Denomination." It will be revealed in a greater light as we continue; trust God! Things that are considered small or little have a tendency to want to carry a big stick, so to speak, in what they say and do. The Little Syndrome carries a complex and a need to be heard as one who has the power. Seeking the attention of everything on site in order to later influence its surroundings. The main objective is to control everything on site to make up for a self-lack of some sort. The reverse psychology is that one small minority that's so-called in control or of power couldn't oppose much of a threat; it could be overthrown if it were to get out of hand. The concept is to win the votes of those considered "Bigwigs" on their team in order to bring others in or on. How many times have we allowed little things to go by without tidying up on them, and before you know it's out of hand? Then, A little becomes a lot on a negative note. The Bible says that it's the little foxes that spoil the vine. (Songs of Solomon 2:15).

L et us pause for a minute. And I can't wait to go further in order to tie in The Book of Revelations in a greater light. We've been considering The Book of Daniel more because of its more details. But we will see the parallel between the two as we go along. Thanks, In Advance, Derrick.

Revelations Pt.7 can't.

Memory Scriptures: Danial 9:1-7, 1 John 5:1-3, 3:18-24.There's much said in these passages that set the stage for how important God's Covenant was established on Mt. Sinai. The Covenant overall lets us know two things that are inevitable. We should be willing to die for the covenant that identifies us to Jehovah in His likeness. Or we will die for not keeping the covenant because of the separation from Jehovah. There's more to be said and taught on the covenant, which can increase our level of confidence, which I'll share as we go along. But, one thing to know about the covenant is that God's Best is ours because He states, "What's Mine Is Yours." Jas. 1:17,18. The Covenant is us stepping down from our rule ship in our lives (On the throne or our hearts)and making a decision to give our will over to the care of God. We're saying, "Lord, take my life in full. I've made a mess of it, and I trust you to be my wheel from here on!" This attitude, first and foremost, before we do anything, will bring God on the scene in our lives through the person of Jesus. 2 Chron. 7:14,15. The enemy works hard at keeping those of us from keeping this mindset because he knows it's what keeps God in the driver's seat. Rev. 12:17. Dragon: Satan, The devil. Rev. 12:9. The woman; The True Church.

Rev.12:17.....and went to make war with the remnant of her seed (K.J.V.).The word "remnant" is a word that brings to mind sowing and using patterns. We use patterns of many sorts that are cut out to make what we desire. And that material that's not used after cutting out or the desired amount is what is called the remnant. The remnant is what's left of the original pattern. That which remains or is left over. So, In short, The devil was wroth, Furious or very angry with the body of believers who were around at the last or closing of this earth's history. Those who were on fire for the Lord were speaking the truth in love at any cost. Those of us who weren't lukewarm symbolize those in the church who will fold under pressure. Those who bear the resemblance of the tare. Matt. 13:37 - 43.

......four great beasts came up from the sea, each different from the other. Dan. 7:3.

Sea; Waters - Rev. 17:15......The waters which you saw where the harlot sits are people, multitudes, nations, and tongues. Dan.7:15, I Daniel was grieved in my spirit within my body (We're spirits, and we possess a soul and live in a body; Our earthly suit), and the visions of my head troubled me. 16th v. I came near to one of those who stood by and asked him the truth of all this. So he told me and made me know the interpretation of these things: v.17. Those great beasts which are four are four kings which arise out of the earth.19th verse: Then I wished to know the truth about the fourth beast which was different from all the others, exceedingly dreadful, with teeth of iron and its nails of bronze, which devoured, broke in pieces, and trampled the residue with its feet, 20th verse, and the ten horns that were on its head and other horn which came up, before which three fell, namely, that horn which had eyes and a mouth which spoke pompous words, whose appearance was greater than his fellows. This fourth kingdom had all the right things to say to win the votes of many. It was eloquent in speech. Smooth like fine oil. (Prov.5:3-5,). Its appearance captivated a live audience, so to speak, and got the attention of all who looked upon it. (Gen.3:6, Ezek. 28:12,13).

21st. verse- I was watching, and the same horn was making war with the saints, and they prevailed against them. 22nd.Until the Ancient of Days came, and judgment was made in favor of the saints of the Most High, and the time came for the saints to possess the kingdom. In the fullness of time, an outward showing will be that God's Church will reign openly. The Lord is doing a mighty work under- ground, so to speak, and at a slow but steady pace because He wants all of us to come to a place of repentance."Hell" is only reserved for the backsliding angels that rebelled at the beginning and Lucifer, who became Satan. (Dan.7:15-22 compare Rev.17:9-14).

Dan.7:23.....The fourth beast shall be a fourth kingdom on earth which shall be different from all other kingdoms, and shall devour the whole earth.25th verse-He shall speak pompous words against the Most High, shall persecute the saints of the Most High, and shall intend to change times and law. Some translations say, "Think to change times and law." This simply means that the changing of things that this 4th power proposes won't influence The True Church. The change is already in effect as we speak, but there are those of us who haven't bit the fruit of its poison by knowing the truth. We know that God is the same today, tomorrow, and forever, and His Will is perpetual. And He's against anything that tries to change His System. (Matt. 5:17-20, Rev. 22:18, 19). We read the 4th power devouring the saints, which is a terrible thing for any and everyone who does so because God will eventually cut them to treads! (Ps. 105:12-15).

Revelations Pt.7 can't; Revelation is a book that gives us history, current affairs, and a printout of things to come. There are prophetic numbers that give us a precise account that comes close to letting us know the season in order to line up. But, as Jesus says in The Gospels, He doesn't even know the time of that hour. (Matt. 24:36). The conditions will be like doing Noah's Days, where the people of Noah's time didn't put stock in what he was saying because, overall, they were trying to figure things out with head knowledge instead of their gut feelings. I say this because, on a simple note, Noah was building a large boat far from the water on dry land, which I know caused them to think Noah was off his rocker. And to see how long of a time he preached to not see his message unfold allowed them to doubt. But God is not slack concerning His promise to us. (2 Pet. 3:8 - 13)

One thing that stuck out the most to me in the story of Noah is the very fact that under pressure, he stayed focused and even though no one heeded God's Calling through him, he got his family together to meet the turning of a whole new world ushered in by the cleansing of water. The three most used tools of Satan were in full effect: Lust of the flesh, Lust of the eye, and the pride of life. (1 Jo. 2:16,17). People were too busy filling their pleasures and what seemed healthy in human life, bonding through the institution of marriage. (Matt. 24:37 - 39). The New Testament is full of conditions that add up to the coming of our Lord and Savior. Also, The manner in which The Anti-Christ is setting up camp and what their angle is. (1 Jo. 2:18 - 21). Through these few passages of scriptures, we can see the importance of the anointing in order to stay with the whole truth and nothing but the truth. This is best described as The Spirit of Prophecy. (1 Jo. 2:20, 21, Compare - Rev. 19:9, 10, 1:9). I propose a few questions, which are also found in the bible study I've shared with many on Revelations in the past. There are two reasons why St. John was exiled to the island of Patmos; what are they? (Rev. 1:9, K.J.V.).What is the testimony of Jesus Christ? (Rev. 19:10). We'll explore more shortly.

Here's" Food For Thought." Let's say over the holidays, one of your best friends comes to visit from out of town and chooses to ride a bus because of conditions on the road that they didn't care to put up with by driving themselves. They told you that their bus would be arriving at ten o'clock on Saturday morning. I asked that you be there to pick them up, and you agreed. So, as you saw, it was getting close to ten o'clock, and you left at a time that would get you there five to ten minutes early, judging by the distance you had to travel from your house. You get there early enough to park and check out the many buses arriving. Ten o'clock arrived, but there was no bus bearing the name your friend was arriving on. You get to wondering whether or not you may have gotten the time of arrival wrong that he or she gave you.

Nevertheless, you go to the front desk to ask what time this bus will arrive, and it is supposed to arrive at ten o'clock, as you were led to believe. But, It just so happens that your clocks at home were set an hour early, which you set all your timepieces by. This means your cell phone, watch, car clock, radio, etc. We can see that even on a small scale, things can be unbalanced, causing confusion until we find out the cause of the problem.

Here's Another situation: Let's say you hear of a major sale that starts on the weekend, Fri. and Sat., on all jewelry at a certain store beginning at midnight on Thurs. You, for whatever reason, waited until the last day of the sale and were under the impression that it was Sat., but it was Sun., the day that the store was closed. You time yourself to get there before 7 p.m. before closing to discover that no one is even in the parking lot. This is because it's the Sun. The day that they're closed. You missed out on the sales altogether because your days got mixed up! We see here that timing is a factor and a tool that gives us the ticket that unlocks what we want and need. This works in the things of God as well.

I've been bringing up past sessions of discussions on the bible prophecy on "Revelations." There's so much that has been shared, which I believe has made a full run in identifying God's Seal vs. Satan's Mark. May we continue to allow the Holy Spirit to have a free course in our lives?

Memory Text: Proverbs 21:2 - Every way of a man is right in his own eyes, But the Lord weighs the hearts.

Luke 11:28 - But He said, "More than that, blessed are those who hear the word of God and keep it!"

Rev.1:3 - Blessed is he who reads and those who hear the words of this prophecy, and keep those things which are written in it; for the time is near.

There's a reward, so to speak, in learning God's Word for ourselves. The scriptures above clarify that. But, Most of all, when we apply it in or to our lives. This is when we can have a breast of the facts to take back territory from false teachings, which were designed to keep us lost. (Hosea 4:6, Prov. 22:28, 27:10). The devil's main objective is to keep us in darkness! He wants to kill, steal, and destroy us. (John 10:10). God's mission is the opposite. He wants to bring life into us and make everything come alive around us (accomplishing our godly goals)by our hands. We are capable of taking back what the devil has stolen. (Job 42:10,11).

The enemy wants to keep destroying everything that's meant for us through Jesus to kill our testimony, which has strength within itself. (Rev. 12:11). The Word of God is powerful and sharper than anything we can imagine. (Hebrews 4:12). That means it can crush all our weaknesses and shortcomings. So, When we associate ourselves with "The Word," we become absorbed by The Word, which totally consumes us! We then become agents of its work in our lives. The Word is alive and is ever-increasing, taking us from glory to glory. It's so important that we understand that The Word is so sacred and completely identifies who God is to where the enemy works even more to discredit its loyalty. This, I mean, is to say that once The Word is gone forth and we step out on it producing faith, God will honor it by bringing our request to pass. We are to live victorious lives here on earth and not just in the sweet by and by, so to speak. (3rd John 2). The Word was hidden from God's people for many years as they worshiped false gods that the earlier generation served (Their forefathers), which was a generational curse. (Ex. 20:5).

But God allowed Josiah to restore everything in God to save the future of God's people. (2 Kings 22:1, 2, 8, 10-13, 23:3, 5-7, 11). The king cleaned up the house so-to-speak, bringing a revival to the land. It's The Word that cleanses us to enable us to walk in the truths of God. It's the washing of The Word! (Ephes. 5:26,27).

The Word washes us, which means it exposes the sin in our lives so we can rid ourselves of it in order to live a holy life. We are allowed to see the shortcomings or mistakes in our lives and walk worthy of the master. The Word is our schoolmaster teaching us to recognize error. God's Word is alive and is always giving birth to things to use as tools to make it in society and to bring a dying world back to God through the Person of Jesus. God's Law is His Word! The Word evolved into the image of God, which is Christ Jesus in the flesh. (John 1:1-5,14). God, The Father, God; The Son, God, The Holy Ghost line up to where there is one, there's the other. Jesus said, "If you've seen me, you've seen The Father." (John 14:9,10). And what's so much more to this is the very fact that if we are in Christ (Through the born-again experience), we are parallel to the three. This means that all things have been placed at our subjection or feet through the authority given by Jesus to us at God's Bidding. So, Then, greater works are at our disposal, according to the next verses. 11-14 of John 14 chp. I said all this to say this: That God doesn't separate Himself from His Word or Law because they are an exact replica of Him. They identify with who He means His Character doesn't change. So, If we learn who God is through His teachings, We can walk the straight and narrow and eat the good of the Land. We can know who He is and be easily detected as His Followers, which is something to strive for. The world can see God for what He really is through us living holy lives. God's Law is His Character, leaving us a pattern to follow. It's His Trademark! Speaking of trademarks, What is Greyhound bus line's trademark? I would trust that you said A greyhound on the sides of their buses, which indicates speed or fastness.

Here's another question: What emblem identifies the state of Texas? A star, which is our seal. The authorities, such as the Texas Rangers, wear this as a badge to let us know that they're in power awarded by the state. And they govern themselves accordingly. It works the same in the things of Christ or God as well. God's trademark is what He stands for, as written in The Ten Commandments. (Ex. 20:1-17). He doesn't stand or tolerate disrespect to our parents (Ex. 20:12), murder (v.13), sex outside of our marriage partner (v.14), and stealing (v.15), just to name a few. The word says happy is he who keeps the law. (Prov.29:18). So, in order to be happy, I must abide by it and not violate it because it is the source of my happiness! I want my life to reflect the character of one who loves the Lord, and that can be done by keeping His Commandments according to what Jesus said. (John 14:15). We'll get into God's Seal verses Satan's Mark for sure as we go on. I thought it would be in this session, but What do I know but to keep doing as I know I'm being led to do

Rev.20:4 - then I saw the souls of those who had been beheaded for their witness to Jesus and for the word of God, who had not worshiped the beast or his image and had not received his mark on their foreheads or on their hands. And they lived and reigned with Christ for a thousand years.5-But the rest of the dead did not live again until the thousand years were finished. This is the first resurrection.6-Blessed and holy is he who has a part in the first resurrection.

We can read here in these passages of scriptures that those who had lost their lives were also those who took a stand against the devil and all that he stands for. It specifically says that they were witnesses for Jesus and, secondly, for the word of God. So, It clearly lets us know that being a witness for Jesus and the word of God are one and the same, or both were and are a reason to be at odds with the devil. This is what made them a target for Satan and for us as fellow believers as well. These witnesses are also of those of us who didn't 1. Didn't (And to us living who are in Christ) worship the beast, 2. Didn't worship his image, 3. Didn't receive the enemy's mark on their forehead, 4. Didn't receive the enemy's mark in their hand. We can see here that 1-4 are ways to avoid missing the 1st. resurrection, which is the ticket to "The New Heaven and Earth."Those who make the first resurrection are stamped as blessed and holy. (Verse 6).

The latter part of verse 6 reads: Over such the second death has no power,.....

So, Those of us who are on the Lord's Team are those of us who act out 1-4, Were called blessed and holy, and had power over what was called.

"The Second Death".This implies that there's a life after one has died, and the life they lived on earth left a pattern or witness that will determine whether they will stay alive after their first death. Let's look into the scriptures to see what "The Second Death" is because we would want to be exempted from it and be given power over it, and it does not have power over us.

Rev.20:14 - Then Death and Hades were cast into the lake of fire. This is the second death. So, we see here that Death (Those who suffered death) and Hades (Meaning the grave and those who were victims who were buried in the grave) were thrown in a pool of fire. These are one and the same that didn't act out 1-4 spoken of earlier. 15- And anyone not found written in the Book of Life was cast into the lake of fire. So, Those who didn't act out 1-4, who didn't make the first resurrection, who didn't have power over the second death, who were thrown in the lake of fire and weren't considered holy and blessed were not in the Lambs Book of Life as well!

Supportive Scriptures: John 5:24- Most assuredly, I say to you, he who hears My word and believes in Him who sent Me has everlasting life, and shall not come into judgment, but passed from death to life. 25- Most assuredly, I say to you, the hour is coming, and now is when the dead will hear the voice of the Son of God, and those who hear will live. 28- Do not marvel at this; for the hour is coming in which all who are in the graves will hear His voice 29- and come forth- those who have done good, to the resurrection of life, and

those who have done evil, to the resurrection of condemnation. The resurrection of condemnation is "The Second
Death" and The Lake of Fire, which we want to miss. Verse
30-...My judgment is righteous,...

We are getting closer to God's Seal vs. The Mark of the Beast.
Until then, Bear with me God's Seal is what The Father can
be identified with. It's His Covenant that binds us to Him.
And we know that through The Person of Jesus, we are
bonded to our God, whose "Jehovah" is to us as well. So,
That very well lets us know that God's Seal is something that
is exercised in the character of Jesus and is passed down to
us as fellow believers. "Love" is what motivates us to live our
lives acting out our love by abiding by "The Covenant." The
Covenant kept our forefathers safe from hurt, harm, and
danger as long as they abide by it.

This is putting God first in all their affairs so they could eat
the good of the land. (Deu. 28th Chp., Exodus 20:1-17). The
Covenant is a "Promissory Note" that God presented to us to
allow the fellowship to stay afresh between Him and us. It
never changes! We may change, but What it does for us and
the consequences for not upholding it remains an infinity.
God said that He'll never leave us or forsake us. He says
even until the ends of the earth or our last walks in this life.
He says in this Covenant, which is a"Marriage License," for
better or worse. He's married to the backsliders! He says our
enemies will be our footstools! But, Most of all, we're with
Him in "Paradise." Let Us not escape reality! Many of us
want the best in this life, but it comes with a price. Not that
we can earn our way into heaven, but we must be obedient
because of the love that compels us. Everything God
promises us is "Covenant Talk," but It's activated by His Seal
upon our lives, which is an "Identifying Mark" that sticks out
among all who claim eternal life. Let Our love be an action
that speaks louder than words! I hope and pray that all this

will arouse us to get to the good part or know our actions, which determines if we have God's Seal! Believe me, God's Seal has been scrutinized, and Satan has carbon-copied it to mislead The Body of Christ!

Memory Text: 2 Kings 5:1 - Now Naaman, commander of the army of the king of Syria, was a great and honorable man in the eyes of his master because by him the Lord had given victory to Syria. We can see here that Naaman had the vote of his king as one to be highly esteemed. And this is because The God of the Hills, Jehovah, allowed it to be. We should know that Syria wasn't an ally of Israel but an enemy of theirs. The only time that God would allow Israel to be subject to their enemies is when they fall out of His Will. Disobedience is what got them enslaved by their adversaries. They became a thorn in their flesh, so to speak. God chastens us because He loves us. It may seem uncomfortable at the time, but this action stems from our decision-making. Our free will policy is that God will not overrule because this is how He framed things in the beginning. To overrule our decision-making is to draw back from His Character. This is not the nature of God! It's like the law of gravity that's been set in motion; what goes up must come down. God is not one to say one thing and do the opposite. So, We see here that Israel got themselves in a jam, which led to a victory for their enemy. Israel couldn't be taken by their enemies, so because it was done, they gave favor to Naaman, who led that victory. We see here God using Syria to buffer His Disobedient,......the Lord had given victory to Syria.

Verse 2- And the Syrians had gone out on raids and had brought back captive a young girl from the land of Israel. She waited on Naaman's wife.V.3 - Then she said to her mistress, "If only my master were with the prophet who is in Samaria! For he would heal him of his leprosy." V.4- And Naaman went in and told his master, saying," Thus and thus said the girl who is from the land of Israel."We see here that through the voice of one little girl (A remnant), God was establishing a restoration for His People. Naaman listened to his wife, who listened to the little girl, and Naaman told the king exactly what he was told. He was desperate or determined enough to seek out the information given.so He asked for permission from the king. You know, in the rest of the story, Naaman went out to pursue his healing and found out that through the prophet Elisha, He had to do specifically like the prophet told him to receive his healing.2 Kings 5:10. Naaman (Like many of us) expected his blessing to come in a certain way, which was totally different from his fantasy.2 Kings 5:11, 12. God's Way is not our way! As far as the heavens are from the earth! Isaiah 55:8, 9. We don't have to understand it all in the beginning, but trust whose voice is revealed to us as God, and He'll make it Plainer as we walk through it. We have to first cast out a reel of faith in the waters of blessings and healing first! Then, Watch the blessings bite to plenty to where our spiritual nets almost break! God gives us a specific way to avoid being labeled as those who will be thrown into the lake of fire. Those who receive the mark of the beast. And just like it seemed useless to do it as instructed by God's messengers, as Naaman thought, we must not be guilty of this in this Final Hour! We can't serve The Lord in any kind of way and expect to make it in. We will clearly see the attributes that have God's approval!

Memory Text: Matthew 5:29- If your right eye causes you to sin, pluck it out and cast it from you; for it is more profitable for you that one of your members perish than for your whole body to be cast into hell. v.30- And if your right-hand causes you to sin, cut it off and cast it from you; for it is more profitable for you that one of your members perish than your whole body to be cast into hell.

Jesus gives us a description of things that can be a part of us, that are tools that aid us in doing wrong. If one were to not denounce these things that violate or jeopardize our relationship with God, It would lead us straight to hell. Jesus suggests that we lose that evil eye or cut off that arm for the sake of saving our souls. This can be easier said than done, depending on how long one has been in the habit of doing the thing that's detestable to God. I'm reminded of Lot's wife, who was so into her possessions and lifestyle she was willing to turn around and go back into sin or back into the city that was on fire. Here, In the story of Sodom and Gomorrah, time was a factor! The destroying angels gave Lot just enough time to gather his family before the city would explode. The heat from the destruction was right on the heels of them, and if one were to even turn to look back, that split second could cause them to be destroyed. This is exactly what happened to Lot's wife. Please believe that she didn't merely look back; her mindset was to go back into the city for selfish reasons. How many of us can identify with this? We claim to have victory over a certain thing or habit to find out in the time of testing, ourselves embracing or going back to that thing that we're weak for. Until we find victory over our bad habits or whatever separates us from God, We'll make a living in hell a reality! Revelations 3:14 let us know that the church was sick and in need and didn't know it until The Spirit brought it to their attention. Then, It was left up to them to take sound advice from the Lord, Rev.3:18- I counsel you...Let Us use these illustrations to keep us out of harm's way! Read The story on Lot. Genesis 19:15-26.

I hope and pray that your days of sharing the Book of Revelations with me have been one of helping us face ourselves and think. I was thinking about what we can do to make a difference with what has been revealed. God is cleaning the temple inside out, which means He's begun with us: The

Church. Our hands are on the gospel plow for a reason. First and foremost, because He's 1st chose us! And we were drawn to Him. Many are called, but Few are chosen. Those who are chosen are those who have accepted The Calling without looking back or to the left or right! It's the Increasing Word! My question is, "Is it increasing in us to the point of looking and sounding more like those who are running to The Battle? I mean knocking down those religious walls of deceit and counterfeit. Kicking over "Sacred Cows so-to-speak! As we get back to closing this message, some may be offended! So, I pray that those who are offended address it to the proper authority in prayer and rebuke! But, As Paul said, "Am I your enemy because I tell you the truth"? Gal. 4:16, John 8:40,41. I can hardly wait til the next session for the sake of sharing "Who's Who." God's Seal of Approval is at stake! I'll hear from you shortly! Let us keep our minds sharp so that we can forever place principles before person-alities.

Church and State: Acts 9:1,2- We can read here and get a clear picture of how the judicial system worked back in the early stages of Christianity. A bill is passed by the church and made a law when the church and state agree. This system is going to be a factor in the final closing of this earth's history. A Certain Church claiming to be the Church of God in Christ (False Church) will have control of the government to pass laws that will outrule many churches that don't worship like they do. This is when the true and ultimate clash will take place. If we don't worship like this Counterfeit Religion, We will be cut off from the state and judicial system having its back. The Church and State Rule is making its way to the top from being secretly underground. This Church System opposes the 1st few commandments, which give God His rightful place and reverence in and by us.

1 Corinthians 15:3- For I delivered to you first of all that which I also received; that Christ died for our sins according to the Scriptures, v.4- and that He was buried, and that He rose again the third day according to the Scriptures, Paul received The Death, Burial, and Resurrection Message, which gave him hope beyond the grave. Jesus came on the scene to present us with a renewed policy. We were no longer subject to death for violating the commandments. This policy allowed us to be put to death by three or more witnesses to be found guilty. Jesus provided a way to bridge the gap between God and man. The work of a high priest through Jesus being a one-time offering for all our sins sealed the deal! The sacrifices of animal blood were no longer needed. Jesus' death symbolizes a way to have peace with God. He became The Way, Truth, and Light (John 14:5). John 14:5-....No one comes to the Father except through Me. How important are The Scriptures? Answer:...v.3 and 4 of 1 Cor. 15......according to the Scriptures,v.5...

The Scriptures are accurate, and The Inspired Word of God.2 Tim. 3:16- All scriptures are given by inspiration of God,...It's our road map to success, giving us signs and symbols for those things that can be considered obscure or not easy to understand. By Jesus raising from the dead, We who are blood-bought can and will have victory over the grave. (1 Cor.15:54....."Death is swallowed up in victory.v.55.....O Hades, where is your victory? Death is the last enemy to be defeated. (1 Cor. 15:26). Then, after death, we face judgment. (Heb.9:27,28). V. 28- So Christ was offered once to bear the sins of many. To those who eagerly wait for Him, He will appear a second time, apart from sin, for salvation. This gives us hope beyond the grave! And as we prepare to see God's Seal, let us embrace it to have peace with God.

As we continue to place principles before personalities, which have been shaped by people, places, and things called our upbringings, let's consider who the ultimate person is who has our best interest at heart. I say this because the people who were in our lives coming up were the ones who showed us an image that was an invitation to life. And I'm hoping that most of their actions were filled with good intentions. But we all can detect what is healthy as our lives go on. In most cases, the people who influenced us the most were in search of their own character in life as well. This is where we form groups to share with those who share the same likes and dislikes as we do, whether they are healthy or not. This is where identities and character begin to shape us for success or failure. Here. We learn to form opinions and social groups that become for or against us. Hate groups are what formed stigmas and stereotypes that could cause riots. These are the many things that have shaped our world, leading up to being what I think is most lethal in the church. We create within us closed minds to things that we don't agree with, along with the people, places, and things that present them. I'm reminded of the movie "Crash," where an opportunity came for the woman who was violated by the officer to be rescued by him, but she was hesitant. All she could think of was the offense by him that stood between her life and death. This could have been tragic, but It became a "Success Story." This happens in the real world as well. But, Keep in mind that it happens only with a being staying open-minded and teachable, which is another meaning for "Humble." Sensitive to The Holy Spirit, which will help us grow along spiritual guidelines continually. So, let us take all of this that's been said into consideration to set the stage for God's Seal. Here We Go! God made us in His own image or likeness to put us on a level where we could understand Him as we resemble Him. Don't we want to resemble Our Heavenly Father? Well, We can see through The Person of Jesus, who's The Expressed Image of God. This means when you've seen Jesus, you've seen The Father. We can't separate the two. We can't find anywhere in the bible where Jesus was doing one thing and The Father setting up a system of doing another. I've chosen my words carefully in saying so because there's a certain impact that will come along with it. The religious leaders of that day and time thought Jesus was the opposite of God, The Father. This was because of not keeping the breast of the facts to keep up with the forecast of change that happened right before their eyes in The Person of Jesus. The long-awaited was dawning on a new day, as the scriptures foretold. However, for whatever reasons, the church wanted to hold on to their own ideals that shaped their church and church leaders. They had the holy writings that gave a full forecast of events that led to Jesus coming on the scene, but they were still not ready! Jesus was The New Kid on the Block who took away the crowd from them. And without a captive audience, prestige and influence didn't shine on them. So, Jesus became a bigger problem than they anticipated. And for those that didn't have a problem acknowledging Him as The Messiah, they didn't like the way Jesus did things, especially after they wanted a king to overthrow the Roman government altogether. They felt like it was a waste because it didn't fit their urge for revenge. This was totally not the character of God! This was an issue then and still is one now, as we will see.

Malachi 3:6- For I am the Lord, I do not change; Therefore you are not consumed, O sons of Jacob. V.7- Yet from the days of your fathers, You have gone away from My ordinances, And have not kept them, Return to Me, and I will return to you.

The Father let the sons of Jacob know first that He doesn't change His way of doing things. He let them know that just like when their forefathers got off track, He gave them space to repent by showing them where they got off track. His actions were not to destroy them immediately but to show them first where they had gone astray. God was saying, "Just like I dealt with your ancestors, so will I deal with you." This has been the case for us as the Church of God in these last days. They had gone away from His ordinances. And He, being the God of second chances, gave them an opportunity to make amends by turning back to Him, which is to repent. It's the nature of God to move with compassion toward us by us first renouncing our sins. They were guilty of not keeping the ordinances. And it works the same today. We are the ones who go astray when God's program of things stays the same. So, since we disconnect from God, we need to show forth an action of returning.

James 4:8- Draw near to God, and He will draw near to you.

Here, we see a first act on our part before God does the same in return. It's His nature!

Malachi 3:7..."But you said, In what way shall we return?" God told them that in the area of their finances, they were missing the mark and that they were considered a curse for doing so (3:8, 9). God was addressing them in the area of their pocketbooks. We are required to be faithful stewards (managers) of what God has trusted us with. (1 Cor. 4:1, 2).

You see, if we, as the people of God, honor Him with our monies, we've passed the ultimate act of loyalty on to God. Then, Everything else lines up properly. The love of money will serve rightfully with its many uses and counterparts. We'll be faithful to sharing, and God will give us more responsibility for even people, places, and things. God keeps the enemy in check for our sake because we honor Him with our money gifts (v.11). V.16- Then those who feared the Lord spoke to one another, And the Lord listened and heard them; So a book of remembrance was written before Him For those who fear the Lord And who meditate on His name. This shows that the name of God is followed by affirmative actions that point to who He is. Example: The Ten Commandments best describes who God is....So, a book of remembrance was written before Him. V.17- "They shall be Mine," says the Lord of the host, On the day that I make them My jewels. And I will spare them As a man spares his own son who serves him." V. 18- Then you shall again discern Between the righteous and the wicked, Between one who serves God and one who does not serve Him.

Malachi 4:1- "For behold, the day is coming, Burning like an oven,......And the day which is coming shall burn them up,".....v.2- But to you who fear My name, The Sun of Right-eousness shall arise With healing in His wings; And you shall go out.....

This lets us know that in that final hour, the Lord will cause us to rise by the healing in Jesus' wings to triumph over the wicked. (v.3). All this is a chain reaction from God being trusted to stand in The Day of Judgement. God compels us to remember The Law of Moses (The Ten Commandments). It says with its statutes and judgments. (v. 4). V. 5- Behold, I will send you Elijah the prophet Before the coming of the great and dreadful day of the Lord. This means, in the spirit of Elijah, not seeing death and doing great exploits for The Lord. Remember, Don't forget what we are compelled to do. This lets us know that there is a good chance that forgetting the Law of Moses can become a reality. James tells us ....v.1:22-But, be doers of the word, and not hearers only, deceiving yourselves.v.23-For if anyone is a hearer of the word and not a doer, he is like a man observing his natural face in a mirror; v.24- for he observes himself, goes away, and immediately forgets what kind of man he was. This is saying that a person who doesn't apply what he or she knows to be of God is like a person who has forgotten what he looks like. In other words, The Content of One's Charac-ter. Be who you say you are by the way you live! Those who remember will be those of us who haven't lowered the standards of God by following false doctrines. We will see what it means to remember the saving of the soul, to be labeled with God's Seal.

Memory Text: Proverbs 18:19- A brother offended is harder to win than a strong city,......

Gal. 4:16- Have I therefore become your enemy because I tell you the truth?

2 Timothy 2:15- Be diligent in presenting yourself approved to God, a worker who does not need to be ashamed, rightly dividing the word of truth. V.24- And a servant of the Lord must not quarrel but be gentle to all, able to teach, patient,v.25-in humility correcting those who are in opposition, if God perhaps will grant them repentance, so that they may know the truth, v. 26- and that they may come to their senses and escape the snare of the devil, having been taken captive by him to do his will.

We, as the people of God through The Person of Jesus, are on a mission to avoid being influenced by things of the world. This, I mean, is the way the ungodly view how life should go. Example: "If it feels good then, do it; "Get all you can while you can then, sit on the can, "Big sin, little sin, etc. These are just a few ways a worldly mentality governs itself. This attitude stems from these scriptures best described: 1 John 2:15- Do does not love the world or the things in the world. If anyone loves the world, the love of the Father is not in him. V. 16- For all that is in the world- the lust of the flesh, the lust of the eyes, and the pride of life- is not of the Father but is of the world. We must resemble The Father in what we do and say. We must be about our Father's Business! It's not popular in the world mainly because it requires one to change and give up its license to sin. There will be those among us who walked with us in the past who will depart from us because of our convictions to go higher in the things of the Lord. (Mark 6:3-....So they were offended at Him. V.4-But Jesus said to them:

> "A prophet is not without honor except in his own country, among his own relatives, and his own house."

We have to be careful how we honor or represent God through The Person of Jesus. In the last lesson study, I asked if there was a commandment that stated specifically, "Don't Forget." The answer is "Yes." Here shortly, we will review this in order to move on to our close. Thanks for listening.

John 7:65- And He said, "Therefore I have said to you that no one can come to Me unless it has been granted to him by My Father." V. 66- From that time, many of His disciples went back and walked with Him no more.

Matthew 7:26- "But everyone who hears these sayings of Mine, and does not do them, will be like a foolish man who built his house on the sand: v. 27- and the rain descended, the floods came, and the winds blew and beat on that house, and it fell. And great was it's fall.".....And great was its fall, which literally means that all one's time and talents were put into a work that didn't stand the natural issues that come with everyday life. When it came to the time of testing, the project couldn't pass security standards. It lacked the right formula, which was hearing and applying what one had been taught. Great was that fall based on the fact that they put everything they had into the project; that was a failure. The more effort, the greater the fall or loss! This lets us know that hearing is half the battle. We must follow through with affirmative action. We must have a strong finish. This race of life goes to those of us who will endure to the end. There's not much emphasis put on one's beginning in comparison to one's finish. It matters to get started first in this race of life. In this race of life, as a believer, everyone is a winner! It doesn't matter who crosses the finish line first to last. We just need to finish the race to be a winner! To be counted as those who have a right to the Tree of Life. Now, God's Blueprint requires us to give homage to Him first and then to our fellow man. (Matt 22:37-40).

Matt. 22:37- Jesus said to him, "You shall love the Lord your God with all your heart, with all your soul, and with all your mind." v. 38-This is the first and great commandment. What was Jesus saying when He made this statement? He was saying that we should love God with our whole being without leaving anything out. In doing so, we would have kept the first four commandments written in Exodus 20:1-11. This is the first and greatest commandment because it puts God first in our lives. Matt. 6:33- But seek first the kingdom of God and His righteousness. v. 39- And the second is like it: "You shall love your neighbor as yourself." (Exodus 20:11-17) v. 40- On these two commandments hang all the Law and the prophets."What was Jesus saying here? If you love your fellowman or another human being, such as your parents, you would honor them (obey them), not lie to one another, steal, or even kill them. You would treat them like you would want to be treated. So, Jesus explained the ten requirements of God differently. Nothing was taken away from them or added. He told them that The Law and the prophets lived out their lives honoring this creed. (V.40). Out of all these choice attributes of the Lord given to us on Mt.Sinai and spoken by Jesus when asked which were the greatest, the # 4 Commandment was asked to not forget.

Memory Text: Matthew 12:25-.....Every kingdom divided against itself is brought to desolation, and every city or house divided against itself will not stand. This is what Jesus told them, as He knew what they were thinking after He had cast out a demon. He explains to them that working against one another will defeat its purpose. Let's Keep in mind that the number one strategic move since the very first war was to divide and conquer. This is the strategy the enemy uses on us through denominations. God never intended for us to characterize ourselves by placing labels on people, places, and things such as denomination does. But How else were we to identify Christ-likeness? We are encouraged to be holy like God, who has called us through The Person of Jesus. This is in our conduct or the way we are towards everything we come in contact with. 1 Peter 1:15-17. It goes on to say that God judges our actions here on earth and that it would be in our best interest to be found of honor to God......., "Be holy, for I am holy." This means following God's Pattern, and we can do this by following Jesus' footsteps as the disciples did, as found herein.

Acts 13:42- So when the Jews went out of the synagogue, the Gentiles begged that these words might be preached to them the next Sabbath. v. 43- Now, when the congregation had broken up, many of the Jews and devout proselytes followed Paul and Barnabas, who, speaking to them, persuaded them to continue in the grace of God. V. 44- On the next Sabbath, almost the whole city came together to hear the word of God. Acts 17:2- Then Paul, as his custom was, went into them, and for three Sabbaths reasoned with them from the scriptures,v.3-explaining and demonstrating that the Christ had to suffer and rise again from the dead, and saying, "This Jesus whom I preach to you is the Christ."This gives us steps to follow, which man has fallen from. The 4th Commandment starts out by saying, "Remember"! Meaning, Don't forget! God put it in writing with His Finger of Love when he gave The Commandments to Moses. (Exodus 31:18, 32:15, 16). This is the only place where we can find in the bible where God literally wrote The Scriptures. The rest of the

Holy Word was entrusted by holy men. How important should that be to us? Very important!

Let's give an account of how things were set up in the tabernacle or temple. The Ark of the Covenant, also called The Covenant Box, was placed in The Most Holy Place, also called The Holies of Holies. The Ten Commandments, also called the tablets of the covenant (Deu. 9:9, 11), were placed inside The Covenant Box, which symbolizes the bond or covenant that God had made with us by keeping The Commandments. And on top of the Ark of the Covenant was the Mercy Seat along with the Two Cherubim. (Exodus 25:10 - 22). Read Ex. 26:33 - 35, 31:12 - 18. To-Be-Con't.

I would like to conclude that this is my contribution to A Study or Examination of God's Revealing of where this existing world is at in The Closing of This Earth's History. I also added some material that seem fitting to refresh our minds, along with a short bible study. Thanks for giving this lesson a chance as we keep an open mind, Pastor Derrick Lacy.

Today is the best day of my life because Jesus lives big in me today. This is one of my favorite sayings that has been with me since I first got saved in 1982, right after my first child was born, Cory Lynn Lacy (Coconut). This saying was passed on to me from Bro. Kenneth Copeland. More and more, it has the ability to help me identify with it on a more personal level. So, I say and think this every day that I'm blessed to see another day, which is another day that I can correct the past if it was a day of gloom. I encourage whosoever to put it in your diet things and let it grow inside you and swell up to encourage you to be the strong spiritual giant that the Lord intended you to be. And remember, God's best is yours; that's why Jesus paid it all!

This shout goes to those who truly know that a life without direction can lead to open doors leading to an undesirable path. Note: If we don't know who we are and who we are, we can't determine our destination. Let identity crisis be far from us as God's creation. And remember, We're either allowing things to happen or making things happen, whether neg. or positive. Enjoy the event, and Happy Sabbath! God's Day

Isaiah 58:13,14,59:1,2

Everybody has their own definition of every word found in the webster. For instance, Success to some may be as small as not getting into an argument with people, places, or things just for the day. My question is, what does God have to say about it in any subject matter? Here's where searching the scriptures comes into effect. This is where many of us fail to look it up for ourselves and choose to go by what someone else says about this or that. We are to work out our own soul salvation with caution according to the holy word. We are compelled to study to show ourselves true to the calling of The Most High. So, Let's get our spiritual feet wet and quit holding on to the banks of past failures. Let Us plunge into the deep in order to keep us from trusting in our own abilities. This can and will hinder us from trusting God totally to stunt our growth. We must grow along spiritual guidelines to get to points A and B in order to receive more from God. Let Our cups run over; It's up to us! All things revolve around God's Timing, which is always on point; Perfect! We arrive at a place or state of status based on the decisions we've made yesterday or in the past. This was done based on what we thought and acted on. So, Let us be careful to make every move a calculated step. This is because they come with consequences and conditions. Remember, the way we spend $1 is the way we'll spend $10. And the way you spend $10 is the way you spend $100. Let Us major in minors.

May we continue to not grow weary of doing God's Will because if we do not give up or give in, we'll see the rewards. Remember, a little is a lot to someone who's without. And in order to truly keep what little bit we have, we must give it away! Let us be faithful over a few things to major in minors. Amen!

PART TWO

CHAPTER 9
A WHOLE NEW WORLD

While learning to dance to your tunes, I know you've taken into consideration that I'm likely to step on your shoes, which could throw us offbeat. So, be patient with me. I'll catch on sooner or later for the benefit of both of us. Ours could be Partners for Life with room to grow, seeing that you live up to your name(A Whole New World). This will be the closest thing to perfect that one has ever seen! The news will travel far, based on our success level, that can happen at a rapid pace, not exceeding the speed limit but with small amounts of adrenaline applied at its proper timing. All this makes for a good sandwich w/a shake and fries! I'm confident in this very thing based on my level of determination and enthusiasm. Yes, This zeal we have will take us far, even to the top. I'm learning more and more that practice makes perfect, which compels me to continue trusting in the moves of training that I fully don't understand. You teach that caring is sharing, and this has been quite a test for me after being in relationships that take and never replace, not even on a small scale. So, May this practice take wings in my growth so I can soar high with a bird's eye view. To-Be-Con't.

I'm thankful that we have and serve a God of second chances! I'm reminded that one of our great leaders in biblical history, "Moses" was in need of a second chance because he messed up. The Bible says everyone born of a woman would suffer in this life from shortcomings (Paraphrased). Moses was brought up from good stock and went to the finest of schools, which even taught him a second language, which enabled him, for the long haul, to better communicate with those in his environment. All this made for Moses to be a good candidate for a great leader, which was "God's Perfect Plan" for his life. We can learn a lot from Moses' experience, which the bible encourages us to heed the examples of past bible lessons. 1 Corinthians 10:6,11-13. Moses jumped the gun, so to speak, by taking matters into his own hands and getting emotional. And while he thought no one saw him, He avenged his fellowman out of timing without "The Anointing" on what he did. This act cost the children of Israel 40 years. Extra bondage! This affected or hindered the move of God and His people, but It didn't stop"God's Plan of Action." God gave Moses a second chance and allowed him to redeem himself. Moses' fellowman lashed out at him verbally in the matter of killing the Egyptian soldier. The fellowman said, "Who put you in charge? And if I don't agree to what you're asking of me, will you kill me too like you did the soldier?"Human nature is prone to bring up one's shortcomings at a time when it may be asked of them to line up because of procrastination. The fellowman went as far as to tell Pharaoh what took place, which in terms got a hit put out on Moses. We later find Moses on the backside of the desert, tending sheep. He had gone on with his life and took on a wife in the process. He was tending his father-in-law's sheep in the area of Mount Horeb. God allowed him a position of leading and caring for something as small or simple as sheep, though one may think. And before he was promoted from this position to leading God's people, Moses had "A Spiritual Awakening."

He was at the right place at the right time! All this time, Moses appears to be still in harmony with God even after missing the mark. I believe this, and it's evident that after seeing the burning bush, He heard the voice of God. In order to hear God speak, one must be in harmony with Him. Moses was curious enough about the burning bush to go investigate. There, he got instructions from God, which put him back on track with God. What a success story that painted a pretty picture for our sake. We who are of The Body of Christ have the same commitment by knowing who we are in Christ. Let Us continue learning who we are by walking in harmony with God.

I woke up this morning with my mind stayed on Jesus. This statement holds true as my confession. It derives from one of our Old One Hundreds from our hymnals. I thought I would take time out to share a revelation that was passed on to me quite some time ago in my early walks with The Lord. We who are professing Christians have taken the initial step in accepting Jesus' Death, Burial, and Resurrection, which covers us as blood-bought. Even though God never intended for there to be denominations in the church, sadly, it shaped and formed to be a common thing in Christendom. And the number one major strategic move that's been exercised since the very first war (Divide and Conquer) raised its ugly head!

Believers allowed themselves to be singled out and caused A Spiritual Holy War against one another. The first rule of thumb (Striving to keep the unity of peace among ourselves) was violated! This left the forces of darkness to have an edge, as we claim to be wise but became fools unaware. So, The church suffered greatly by killing their wounded through closed-mindedness and dissociation. The spirit of fault-finding and judging was next to come on the scene. In General, Every denomination has been given a certain revelation from on high (Our Heavenly Father through the channels of The Holy Spirit), which has become the cornerstone or foundation (Doctrine) of their church. Without a shadow of a doubt, it was endowed by God, which gives the church every reason to shout and move forward. But, This endowed truth is a spiritual tool or force that the church uses to beat other churches over the head because of their lack of knowledge concerning that certain revelation given.

In conclusion, Every denomination has tasted revelations from God. Example: Baptist doctrine, foundation, cornerstone, etc., is baptism with complete submerging (Head to Toe). Mormons; Church of Jesus Christ Latter Day Saints-They believe in the redemptive work on Calvary through The Person of Jesus. In terms, they hold to being Christ's Church on earth in these last days, putting it lightly. Different facets of the church build their church on revelations of God, which is like having one piece to the puzzle and needing an overall vantage of God's Plan of Salvation. As a suggestion, if the professing Body of Christ would present their endowed truth with the right motives, which can only be done by The Holy Spirit, then and only then can we allow God to move and have His Being in us! We could then bridge the gaps to allow rivers of living water out of us. Read: Isaiah 58 Chp. We could lay our pieces to the puzzle down for examining through and by The Spirit and only by The Spirit (Testing All Things By The Holy Spirit, which we are compelled to do.) By this, we come together with such an anointing as on the Day of Pentecost and truly get the finished work done to usher Christ's Second Advent. Each piece of the puzzle (Revelation Knowledge) would fit into place to be able to get the fullness of God's Plan of Action. Line upon line, precept upon precept!

CHAPTER 10
TODAY'S READING

PROVERBS 3:11,12

Let us invite Our Heavenly Father's Corrections. This lets us know He has our back and we're safe in His hands. No one can pluck us out of His hands when we're in Christ Jesus! Key Word: In Christ Jesus. We must first be in Christ as "New Creatures" to get this benefit through "The Covenant." Then, We can build on not being afraid to make mistakes. This means making mistakes in The Lord. When we make mistakes in The Lord, we can stand to be corrected and grow from them. Mistakes that follow spiritual guidelines keep us from going all out on the deep end. Mistakes that are open to God through forgiveness. This means that we quickly repent and allow healing to flow. Making mistakes in The Lord keeps us from allowing ourselves to take penitentiary chances, so to speak. Why did God put erasers on pencils? Because He knew we were going to make mistakes. "Correction" is The Heavenly Father's Way" of exercising His Love towards us, as strange as it may seem. Our earthly parents or family members use this method (Tough Love) to bring out the best in us. So, how much more does God promote this act of discipline? "Love" is the motivation. Be encouraged!

JEREMIAH 44 HISTORY REPEATED

Jeremiah spoke to the people (His people) of their waywardness that brought them to a place of hitting rock bottom to be oppressed in every area of their lives. Jeremiah, being a mouthpiece of God, delivered a message of reflection, bringing their case before them. This enabled them to face themselves and think. This put them in the judgment seat and led them to see how they had gotten to a place of provoking God to anger. We ourselves can identify with such behavior because we do the same in some shape, form, or fashion in our walk with Christ, behaving in such a way as if we didn't know God at all. One thing leads to another as to falling in rebellion with our certain project of sin that starts out moderately to become full-blown. And before you know it, it wears us down to nothing attractive in the sight of God. By not heeding the warning signs in the early stages of our rebellion, we can't help but continue in sin (Our mess), which takes us on the fast track of destruction like a locomotive that's reached top speed. But these are the things that can and will lead us to repentance (Back to God) to Our First Love. I'm reminded that a little is a lot to have nothing at all. So, we can gradually take back the pureness that was valuable in Christ one step at a time, which is a lot, even when we are allowed baby steps because our hearts are conditioned and driven to fulfill our place with God. So, the generational curses of our forefathers reach a turning point that leads us back to The Father.

THE DAY I OUTRAN GOD

I can remember O so plain that very day. The Good Lord looked one way, and I looked away from Him. This got me a few paces ahead as I sped past the sound barrier, which was surely not seen. As I got to my destination on the other side of the world, I could tell I had not been found. Mainly because the company I embraced didn't acknowledge or even speak of Him. They were all for self and all for change, leaving the mention of His Name. So, there we went, building our own society with me, who was voted in as Chief Executive. Life was much better managed, seeing that less resistance was our reward. Never a mention no more of the likes of His Character to put us to an open challenge thought to help in growing to betterment. There was no need to because all was well. That's how I outran God!

THE RIGHT ARM OF GOD

2 Tim.2:15,16

We are compelled to get to a place of maturity to rightly administer truth, not mere truth, but the whole truth in the light of the scriptures. This implies that we can meet God's approval, and surely, this comes about by trusting Him with all things from the least to the greater. It's a good thing to be in a place where you can share the truth and not offend people. Be it known, not everyone will accept the truth that may be shared, which requires proper timing, which only The Holy Spirit can give. To operate in such a way to share the truth about anything, for that matter, is a skill that has to be developed. But God has entrusted us as followers to handle such a task. To be able to put the truth in a position of being received with gladness is rightly dividing it, so to speak. Knowing is half the battle, but let us be able to know what we are saying by saying what we know. This is to be in a position to not let others entrap us because we don't have the breast of the facts. The 16th verse encourages us to stay clear of talks and conversations that aren't life-threatening. Things that don't promote positive results. It gives us a reason to avoid profane things because it can and will influence us to take it to the next level of more ungodliness. This letter of Timothy assures us that the necessary steps can be used or exercised to keep vulgarity from increasing. We have it within us to bear arms of righteousness to be awarded as highly favored by God. Continue with well-doing followers of Christ.

WARNING BEFORE DESTRUCTION

Jer.26:1-6

Here in the scriptures, we read a message summoned by the prophet of God. He went to the household of faith to announce what God had fashioned for them. God's Love for us crosses boundaries that mere man wouldn't endure to get our attention. Truly, God looks beyond our faults to get us back under the umbrella of protection.

The prophet was told to go to the meeting place of the saints to expose them to the whole truth and nothing but the truth. The Lord advised him to leave nothing out in so many words. There's a place in Christ that puts us in a position of protection that comes through obedience. It allows The Hedge of Protection that covers us and keeps us from hurt, harm, and danger. We can be confident of this very thing: if God is for us, who cares who's against us? It was questionable as to whether or not the message would fall on the hearers in such a way as to bring them out of their stupor.

Sometimes, the conditions of one's heart and the depth of the tragedy can and will determine if we will accept the deliverance granted to us. But, we can rest assured The Father will send a prophet or messenger. We just need not shoot the messenger but, rather, heed the calling to restore us back to sanity.

MARK 13:28-31 THE PARABLE OF THE FIG TREE

We can learn a lot by observing nature, which is God's gift to us. This implies that God created all things perfect, which gives us a pattern to identify things that may be obscure or not quite plain to understand. The fig tree is a figurative of life to determine times. This illustration is in reference to the 2nd Return of Christ to totally take back what was stolen. The ability to live accident-free under no false pretenses. We are to observe nature in such a way that we get a carbon copy of Christ's Return so as not to fall short. This lets us know that all things reproduce after themselves in an inexcusable time frame for us not to be prepared. There will be A Great Falling Away in the forecast for today's history, giving us a heads up to soul search. Truly, His Coming is At The Door!

Let us be prepared, people, to secure our salvation so that we can lead others before it's too late. Be Encouraged.

MOTIVES

Jer.22:1-6,11-17

We read here in the Word of God addressing the church to walk with integrity toward those who are downtrodden. This requires motives that are given freely. As the scriptures let us know, judgment will begin with us, the Body of Christ. It goes on to warn through the prophet Jeremiah, recalling the history of the fallen nature of a leader to keep it from being A Repeat. We do well to guard ourselves from selfish motives that can lead to entrapment to dishonest gains. For what would it profit us to win the world and lose our soul? What do we value the most? As for my house and me, we choose the Lord!

GAL. 5:1 FREEDOM ALL OVER

How many of us can identify with being free more than just on One Level? This is to say that there are many of us who have been locked up in jail and on to prison. This is a type of bondage that will put A Damper on even basic necessities and how much as well as what a person can have at the time. A prisoner has been placed in an environment that is far from them, being able to walk away from unfavorable crowds based on how he or she is housed. There are a lot of privileges that one takes for granted in society that are not at one's disposal, such as choosing one's own time when one wants to go somewhere to experience A Five five-star meal of some sort. I can go on and on about this area of bondage, but there are others.

Forms of Bondage one may behold that come from being in broken relationships can keep us from moving forward in life when the opportunity presents itself. This can be because being in situations long enough to become a habit turned hazardous because we didn't heed the warning signs. And sometimes, it may take longer to reverse The Curse than the time put into a thing. But there's hope in Christ and learning how to accept and exercise The Word that has pardoned us through Jesus. Jesus paid it all, and through Him, we have the know-how to walk down the problems that come to smother us. Through Jesus' Redemptive Work on Calvary, we can take back what we allowed to be stolen. Our minds carry our decision-making to a place of refuge. The scriptures tell us that it's possible and A Reality in Christ who releases us, but we must determine in ourselves by accepting it by An Act of Receiving it. It also lets us know that we can choose to get back into a rut willingly or unawares. Let us be careful to guard ourselves from things that we cherish that become idols that hold us captive against our will or better judgment. Good Day.

THE SEVEN NAMES OF THE LORD

Jehovah-Jireh: The Lord will provide. *Genesis 22:14*

Jehovah-Rapha: The Lord that healeth. *Exodus 15:26*

Jehovah-nissi: The Lord our banner. *Exodus 17:15,16*

Jehovah-shalom: The Lord our peace. *Judges 6:23,24*

Jehovah-ra-ah: The Lord, my shepherd. *Psalm 23*

Jehovah-tsidkenu: The Lord our righteousness. *Jeremiah 23:6*

Jehovah-shammah: The Lord is present. *Ezekiel 48:35*

PASTOR'S CORNER

I remember when life was much simpler. The birds flew south for the winter, and kids could play outside without being taken by strangers. But as the world turns, we learn that it is made up of good and bad. Families have to make up their minds about whether they will serve God or things of this world. Continue to choose life, which is in Christ, because a life outside of God just exists. Choose today because tomorrow we die. Good Day.

Count The Cost Starting a project based on an idea requires us to count the cost. The cost of doing the research for the proper material to allow the plan to be under construction. We hire laborers to carry out the making of a business. This gives purpose to motivate the cause. As we build on a structure to support our goals, we determine its ability to perform the task at hand. The ability to carry out its order determines how well it will bring a profit. The Art of Network increases its sales. As the company grows, its productivity allows it to build more structures after its own.

THE REAL TRUTH BIBLE STUDY COURSE

1. When will the end-time message spoken of in Daniel be open or revealed? *Dan. 12:9*

2. Would Daniel be alive when the end-time message is active? *Dan. 2:13*

3. Who did the beast and false prophets deceive with their works of magic? *Rev. 19:20*

4. What happens to the ungodly who don't have the seal of God? *Rev. 14:9-11*

5. In the closing of earth's history, what will the beast do.? *Dan. 8:25*

6. What will those who understand the prophecy spoken of in Revelation be called? *Rev. 1:3*

7. Will God keep us equipped to understand His messages? *Amos 3:7*

8. Is the judgment of God honest and righteous? *Rev. 19:2,11*

9. Are we to be prepared to meet Jesus, who is our bridegroom? *Rev. 19:7*

10. What are the good works called in the bible? *Rev. 19:8*

11. Will God judge the good and bad on earth? *Eccles. 3:17*

12. Is there a cause and effect for every action? *Rev. 8:6, 7, 22:6, 18:6, Jude 1:6, 2 Pet. 2:6.*